NEW HAMPSHIRE

ON-THE-ROAD HISTORIES

NEW
HAMPSHIRE

Russell Lawson

Interlink Books

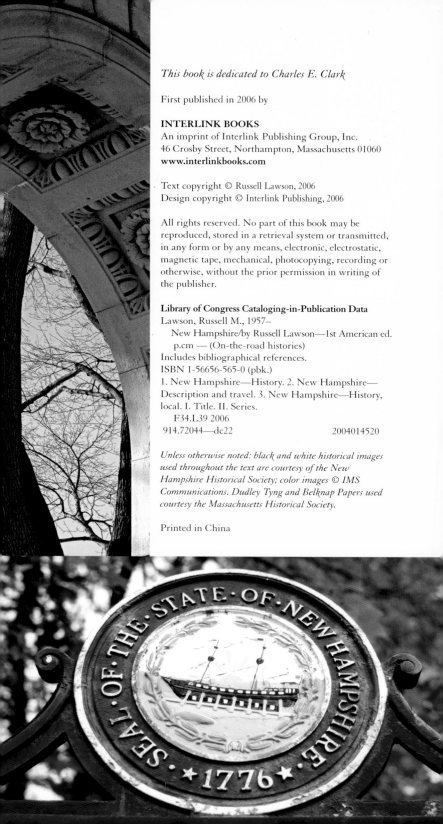

This book is dedicated to Charles E. Clark

First published in 2006 by

INTERLINK BOOKS
An imprint of Interlink Publishing Group, Inc.
46 Crosby Street, Northampton, Massachusetts 01060
www.interlinkbooks.com

Text copyright © Russell Lawson, 2006
Design copyright © Interlink Publishing, 2006

Library of Congress Cataloging-in-Publication Data
Lawson, Russell M., 1957–
    New Hampshire/by Russell Lawson—1st American ed.
    p.cm — (On-the-road histories)
Includes bibliographical references.
ISBN 1-56656-565-0 (pbk.)
1. New Hampshire—History. 2. New Hampshire—
Description and travel. 3. New Hampshire—History,
local. I. Title. II. Series.
    F34.L39 2006
  914.72044—dc22   2004014520

Unless otherwise noted: black and white historical images used throughout the text are courtesy of the New Hampshire Historical Society; color images © IMS Communications. Dudley Tyng and Belknap Papers used courtesy the Massachusetts Historical Society.

Printed in China

CONTENTS

Introduction 7

I. GOD'S PORT 13
The Arrival of Rev. John Tucke—John Newton Meets
Dudley Tyng—Hawthorne on Vacation

II. THE PISCATAQUA VALLEY 41
The View from Route 1—The Trip to Dover
Jeremy and Ruth Belknap

III. FOLLOWING THE PATHS OF RANGERS 73
The Belknap–Cutler Expedition—Mount Washington
Crawford Notch—Artist of the Word

IV. THE CONNECTICUT VALLEY 107
New Connecticut—Dartmouth College
Reverend Belknap's Itinerary, August 1774

V. THE MERRIMACK VALLEY 125
Thoreau's Journey—Massachusetts Pioneers
Signs and Times—New Hampshire Politics
Josiah and Mary Bartlett of Kingston

EPILOGUE: COUNTRY POND 147

Sources   150
Chronology of Major Events   153
Cultural Highlights 155
Special Events and Contact Information 156
Further Reading 157

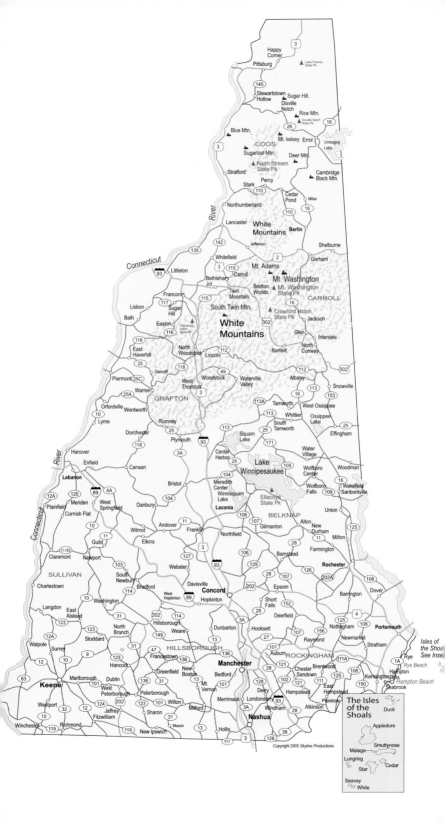

INTRODUCTION

New Hampshire's natural history has shaped its human history. From the rocky Isles of Shoals, six miles out in a cold sea, you can see on a clear day what fishermen four hundred years ago could see: the inland shores, sandy beaches, towering pines, and—appearing like so many clouds upon the horizon—the distant White Mountains, dominated by the grandest peak of the northeast, Mount Washington. Descending from inland mountains, rivers such as the Connecticut, Merrimack, and Piscataqua dictated settlement patterns for the native Algonquin tribes and early English settlers. The first English and European explorers envisioned New Hampshire as a perfect colonial source for fish, timber, and furs. Certainly the earliest settlements at Portsmouth, Dover, Hampton, and Exeter resounded with the sounds of ship builders and sawmills. During the 1600s sporadic conflicts rose between the native peoples and the English colonists. The former, greatly outnumbered, surrendered the land to the latter and moved north to the waters of the St. Francis, in New France. English settlements in New Hampshire nevertheless expanded at a slow rate in the face of cold winters, deep snows, rocky soil, rapid rivers (navigable only by canoe), the dense, reluctant forest, and the White Mountain barrier. The Native Americans, responding aggressively to the many years of European war in America, allied themselves to the French and raided New Hampshire towns and terrorized British-American inhabitants. New Hampshire townsmen formed themselves into militias to defend themselves and to attack the enemy, the most famous example of which was the daring raid of Robert Rogers' Rangers on the St. Francis Indian village in 1759 during the French–Indian War. The Treaty of Paris that ended the war brought peace to New Hampshire, and along with it, the march of frontiersmen and farmers north up river valleys to the foothills of the White Mountains. These were hardy men and women, hardworking, pious, and jealous of their independence and right to act according to what they considered true and lawful. New Hampshirans chose "to live free or die," thereby joining the Revolution against England from 1775 to 1783. New Hampshire was an important source of fighting men and warships. Fortunately for the inhabitants, there were few battles on New Hampshire soil. Unfortunately, trade losses and the curtailing of the fishing industry devastated the local economy—it would take years for New Hampshire to recover from the War for Independence.

When the new U.S. Constitution needed the support of nine of its thirteen states to be ratified, New Hampshire became that decisive ninth state, ratifying the Constitution in 1788, a move which indicated the important role the state would play in political developments during the coming years. President George Washington visited New Hampshire in 1789 and was impressed by the depth and hazards of the Piscataqua River. A decade later the United States founded the Portsmouth Naval Shipyard, which for over two hundred years has had a major impact on the region's economy. Piscataqua merchants took their ships all over the world during the 1800s, and Portsmouth continued to be the trading headquarters for Northern New England. Other cities, however, began to have a leading influence on the economy. Manchester, built around the Amoskeag Falls of the Merrimack River, became an important factory center. Towns such as Newmarket and Dover, once centers of the lumber industry, built massive factories that produced manufactured goods. Meanwhile New Hampshire also produced political leaders such as Daniel Webster, who stood for manufacturing interests, the end of slavery, and democratic values. Abraham Lincoln's much-publicized visit to the Granite state during his 1860 campaign for the presidency indicated the ongoing importance of New Hampshire in American politics.

New Hampshire's most enduring mark during the past century and a half has been on tourism, the arts, and literature. The natural beauty of the sea, forests, and mountains inspired poets such as Robert Frost, who lived in Derry, Celia Thaxter of the Isles of Shoals, Augustus Saint-Gaudens of Cornish, and numerous visitors such as Timothy Dwight, Nathaniel Hawthorne, and Henry

David Thoreau. People from all over the world sought adventure braving the dangers of ascending Mount Washington, tranquility sailing Lake Winnipesaukee, and health relaxing at the Isles of Shoals. Tourism continues to have the dominant impact on the state.

New Hampshire welcomes the inquisitive explorer with inviting routes to the past. Mariners sail the waters from the Piscataqua to the Merrimack rivers while hugging the sandy shore and using the Great Boars Head and Little Boars Head as landmarks. Perhaps they feel, like John Smith, the boat tossed about by the waves, inhale, like Samuel de Champlain, the salty air, and wonder, like Martin Pring, what lies hidden onshore among the stands of white pine. Rivers that fall from the distant highlands to the sea now host motorized craft that push through the swirling currents of the Piscataqua, making light of what was a fierce challenge in the age of sail. The pinnace, gundalow, and schooner once made their way, gently, through the hazards of islands and narrows that mark the mouth of the Piscataqua River. Fiberglass canoes glide upon inland rivers of less force but equal beauty, retracing the path the Penacooks and Pequawkets took in their birch-bark counterparts.

Land routes of the past continue to guide travelers on their voyages of discovery. Ancient animal and Native American traces yielded to the surveyor's compass and road-builder's axe to become roads to the interior. These roads parallel the descending Connecticut River where it marks the western boundary of New Hampshire with Vermont, pierce Pinkham Notch in the shadow of Mount Washington, and trace the indentations of beaches and protrusions of rocky outcrops while hugging the coast. The postal routes of yesterday—the ones that helped General Washington's couriers make quick work of their task and also guided messengers with their epistles of love or notices of suffering and death—became, like Route One, the highways of today.

The names of such roads, highways, and lanes, as well as the towns and cities they connect, and the natural and human landmarks to which they lead, recall New Hampshire's past. Portsmouth patriots dropped King Street for State Street during the War for Independence. After the Revolution,

Fort William and Mary—named for English royalty and guarding Portsmouth Harbor to protect the King's commerce—became Fort Constitution and defended the American Republic. The hamlet of Kingston, however, is still proud to bear the loyalty of its birth in 1694. The town of Laconia borrows its name from the appellation given to wilderness New Hampshire by its first English proprietors, John Mason and Ferdinando Gorges, in the early 1600s. Concord, the state capitol, was the name chosen in 1765 by inhabitants seeking peace after years of property disputes. The Piscataqua and Squamscott rivers recall the native peoples who once made New Hampshire their home before the coming of the English. Kancamagus Highway, which threads its way through the White Mountains, honors a chief of the Penacooks, a descendant of Passaconaway, who himself gave name to a town and a mountain.

New Hampshire is an anachronism, as anyone who visits the state can see. Its people once emerged from a cold Atlantic sea, founded settlements around beaches, harbors, bays, and rivers, and struggled to penetrate dense northern forests and ascend the sublime inland peaks. But today, New Hampshirians seek to distance themselves from relying on the forest, rivers, and sea. The present state of New Hampshire—of interstate highways and turnpikes, state liquor stores, casinos, amusement parks, upscale communities, exclusive prep schools, luxurious condominiums, nuclear power, and high tech computer software companies—accommodates with some hesitation the picturesque colonial ports and villages, old sturdy saltbox houses, and the still wilderness of the north country. New Hampshire has hosted fast and furious economic, social, political, cultural, and technological changes. But travel Route 1A as it winds along the coast, drive Route 150 through the small town of Kensington, walk the paths about Portsmouth harbor, or happily lose your way in the village of Newcastle, and you will discover the most antiquarian of states. History exudes from the old stone walls that have marked property for centuries. The pungent smell of the sea, the cries of gulls overhead, the cold wetness of the fog, the old wharves, narrow streets, ancient houses, old town greens, cemeteries, and three hundred year-old market centers all

Traditional white clapboard New Hampshire church

form a tale of the past, a chronological record, a history without words. Yet words are needed to tell the whole story. They must fill in the gaps of forgotten human experience and support the rotting timbers in order to journey back in time—rather like rummaging through a dusty, forgotten attic to find the mementos of yesterday. It is, then, to yesterday that we return.

1

God's Port

Mariners call "shoal" any rocky or sandy obstruction of the typical depth of the sea, any hazard to boats and to the lives of seamen. The sailor spots the shoal by the distant spray, the uncommon swirling white water that betrays an object just under the surface. Not that shoal water is easy to discover. The surging waves, the crests and valleys, and the continual fluidity of the sea make observation difficult. You have to feel your way about the shoals. The great sailors of the past had a sixth-sense about navigating the unexpected, anomalous sea. They knew there to be an ebb and a flow to the sea, as to life; the best mariner senses the ebb and flow, the rhythmic rising and falling of the deck.

John Newton was such a mariner. He sailed his small boat, probably a fishing shallop, when conditions allowed—when the easterlies weren't bringing the whitecaps to the surface, crashing into the rocks and sending spray everywhere, causing the craggy stones to glisten before the water seeped into the cracks and returned to the sea. Mornings when the sea was like a calm mirror heralded a good day to haul the nets and tackle aboard ship and cast off to the east, and the Banks. On such days the wind would stir soon enough, hopefully from the southwest, though even a contrary breeze, if slight, could propel the boat in the general direction, tacking toward its destination.

John Newton's home was the Isles of Shoals, eight tiny islands in the Atlantic Ocean several miles off the coast of New Hampshire. Today they are a place for tourists and researchers. The Star Island Conference Center welcomes visitors to the delightful repose of island breezes on otherwise hot summer days. Even the most devoted landlubber feels the call of the sea when looking out upon the broad Atlantic from his perch on one of the many rocky outcrops of Star Island.

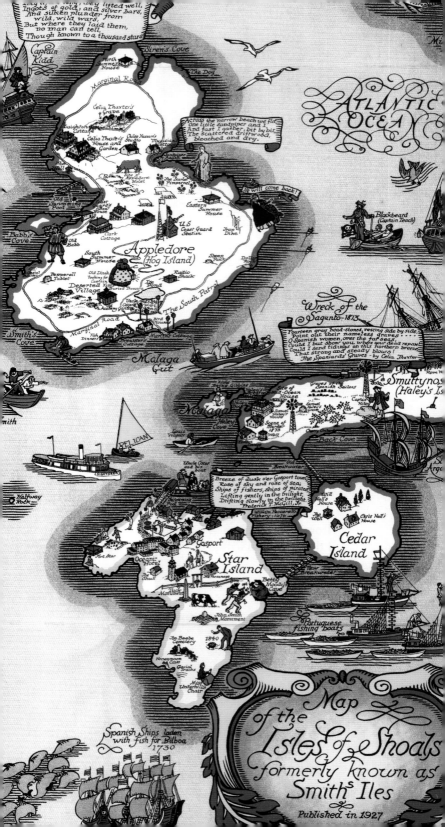

They, they lifted well,
Ingots of gold, and silver bars,
And silken plunder from
wild, wild, wars,
But where they laid them,
no man can tell,
Though known to a thousand stars

Captain Kidd

North Summer House

Siren's Cove

The Dog

Marginal Road

Celia Thaxter's Grave

ATLANTIC OCEAN

Leighton Cottage

Celia Thaxter's Studio

Childe Hassam's Studio

Celia Thaxter's House and Garden

Magician's Cottage

Across the narrow beach we flit,
One little sandpiper and I
And fast I gather, bit by bit,
The scattered red driftwood,
bleached and dry.

The Scarlet Pimpernel

New Appledore Hotel

He will come back!

Eastern Summer House

Blackbeard (Captain Teach)

U.S. Coast Guard Station

Trap Dike

Old Swimming Hole

Babb's Cove

Old Babb

Clark Cottage

Appledore (Hog Island)

Sheep Rock

Dolly Shack

South Summer House

Radio Shack

Pennewell Tablet

Old Dinah Tommy for Captain Buried Treasure

Deserted Village

The Pond

Uncle Oscar's Garden

The South Patrol

Smith's Cove

Marginal Road

Fish Dinner House

Bird Island

Martin Cottage

Brewster's Cottage

Malaga Gut

Wreck of the Sagunto - 1813

Fourteen gray head-stones, resting side by side,
Point out their nameless graves. . . .
O Spanish women, over the far seas,
Could I but show you where your dead repose
Could I send tidings on this northern breeze
That strong and steady blows!
The Spaniards' Graves — by Celia Thaxter

Eben Gibbons' Reef

Graves of Spanish Sailors

Mid-Ocean House

Smuttynos (Haley's Is

Malaga Cove

Samuel Haley's House

Scene of Murder 1873

Well

PELICAN

Back Cove

Uncle Oscar and his boat

Louis Wagner

Halfway Rock

Breeze of dusk o'er Gosport town
Rose of sky and rose of sea,
Ships of Fishers, ships of pirates
Lifting gently in the twilight,
Drifting slowly in the twilight.
Frederick T. McGill, Jr.

William Haversall Fisher - 1676

Will Hall's House

The Well

Chris Hall's House

Gosport

Cedar Island

Port Star

Oceanic Hotel

The Shack

Star Island

The Parsonage

New Breakwater

Betty Moody's Cove

Old Breakwater

Tuck Monument

John Smith Monument

Portuguese Fishing Boats

Joe Beebe Cemetery

1840

Honeymoon Cove

Caswell Tracks

Miss Underhill's Chair

Map of the Isles of Shoals formerly known as Smith's Iles

Published in 1927

Spanish Ships laden with fish for Bilboa 1730

Although the Unitarian-Universalist Association owns the
Conference Center, using it for their varied purposes, Star
Island is still very accessible with cruise ships going to and fro
bringing supplies and tourists. The *Thomas Laighton*, for
example, makes daily voyages to the Isles of Shoals, allowing
tourists to stop off at Star Island. The *Thomas Laighton* is
owned by the Whittaker family; Captain Robert Whittaker,
long time skipper of the *Thomas Laighton* and author of *The
Land of Lost Content*, for many years served as a guide for
tourists interested in learning about the past.

Once, several centuries ago, the Isles of Shoals were the
center of the New England fishing industry. From the early
1600s to the early 1800s, these islands hosted hundreds of
fishermen and mariners, along with their wives and children,
as they engaged in the daily task of rending a living from the
sea. The early settlements on the Isles of Shoals at Hog Island,
Smuttynose, and Star Island were a vanguard in the early
American quest to harvest the plenty offered by the New
World. For the sake of living at the heart of their quest for
fish, fishermen withstood the challenges of the Isles: their
barren landscape, their nakedness to the unending wind, and
their complete dependence on the sea.

The Gorges Banks, many leagues off the coast of Maine,
had attracted fishermen for generations. Long before John
Newton, his father, or grandfather arrived at the Isles of
Shoals, itinerant fishermen—the English from Bristol and
Plymouth, the French from Normandy and Gascony, the
Portuguese from Lisbon, and Basques, Scots, and Spanish as
well—sailed these waters. They filled their boats with fish,
made port at the islands along the coast that stretched from
46 to 43 degrees north, and prepared the fish for market.
Then, in the sixteenth century, Spain dominated Central
and South America, and was making inroads into North
America. The French had explored the North American
east coast, sailed up the St. Lawrence River, and claimed the
land of Quebec—New France. The English, meanwhile,
after initial efforts during the reign of Henry VII, made few
attempts to exploit the lands of what they called Virginia, in
honor of the Virgin Queen Elizabeth I. Elizabeth supported
some generally unsuccessful voyages to America. The
competition for empire and control of the waters for fishing

Detail of 1927 Isles of Shoals map

and islands for makeshift ports heated up after 1600.

During the first decade of the seventeenth century, English sailors such as Bartholomew Gosnold and Martin Pring explored the coast of what would become New England. They took note of several islands standing eastward from the mainland, but were more intent on discovering the rivers and harbors on the mainland that would sponsor English colonies. Meanwhile Henry of Navarre, King of France, seeking to build on the earlier discoveries and settlements of Jacques Cartier, granted the region of North America between 40° and 46° north to the Sieur de Monts. In 1604 De Monts and Samuel de Champlain established a colony at St. Croix, which they used as a base the following year to explore the coast south. On this voyage of 1605 Champlain observed and noted in his journal "three or four prominent islands" to the east.

It wasn't until 1614 that these islands finally had a name: Smith's Isles (sometimes called Smyth's Isles). The intrepid explorer Captain John Smith, who sailed these waters during the summer of 1614, had the vision to see the potential in these rough rocks in the sea. Smith explored the islands, finding them a match for his own hardy, persevering, weather-beaten character. He saw in them the vanguard of the English colonial fishing industry— subsequent years proved him right. The islands were far enough from the coast to be defended from Native American attacks. They had several small natural coves to provide some protection for ships during storms at sea. They were superbly located near the Gorges fishing banks from which fishermen could take great numbers of cod. And the islands had a temperate climate from spring to fall that made endurable if not pleasant the fatiguing work of preparing, salting, and packing fish. After Smith's voyage, and the publication of his *Description of New England* in 1616, English fishermen made Smith's Isles the basis of their seasonable operations, catching haddock during summer months and cod during winter and spring months. After the settlement of the New England coast from Cape Cod to Penobscot Bay during the 1620s, fishermen from Massachusetts, New Hampshire, and Maine used the islands as their base; many decided it made more sense to build shacks to live in so that the fishing, drying, salting, and packing could occur on a daily basis. By this time, 1630, the islands had been renamed *Isles of Shoals* by sailors who went by the experience of the moment, trying to avoid shipwreck in shoal water. Captain John Smith's role in founding the Isles of Shoals of New Hampshire is still remembered by a weathered granite monument standing at the southern edge of Star Island.

For most of the seventeenth century the islands with the greatest population of fishermen were Hog and Smuttynose, the two largest of the eight islands that make up the Isles of Shoals. The pioneering fishermen of the early 1600s who lived year round on the Isles spent their days fishing or drying their catch of the day before, mending nets, and patching boats. Fond of drink, they also used profanity frequently and with gusto. They were concerned with prosperity rather than piety and were generally lonely—few women lived in the hardy conditions of the fishing village. From the beginning the fishermen of the Isles of Shoals were drawn to the Piscataqua River settlements for food, supplies, and companionship. By the mid-seventeenth century, women came to live on these misshapen rocks that lacked even enough soil to host the most adaptable of plants. A few of the islands, such as White, Londoners, Malaga, and Duck, were uninhabitable except to the husband and wife with plenty of potable water, food rations, sturdy lodgings, and patience. Hog, Smuttynose, Cedar, and Star were hardly better, yet larger, and more secure in the harsh marine environment.

Nevertheless by mid century there were up to six hundred fishermen and families experiencing some degree of community life. Shoalers built a brick meetinghouse for town and church purposes. Taverns and marketplaces welcomed night-owls, travelers, and buyers and sellers of goods. Itinerant ministers and schoolmasters taught young and old alike. Prosperous fishermen, captains, and merchants resided in well-furnished brick houses. Ambitious husbands such as Henry Sherburne brought young, sturdy wives—Henry's was Rebecca Gibbins—to live in these romantic dots in the ocean. Three brothers, Richard, John, and Robert Cutt, immigrated from Wales to the Isles and became leading merchants; Richard Cutt owned most of Star Island. After his death, and after the

Star Island, 1800s

formation of the independent province of New Hampshire in 1692, there was a general exodus of Shoalers to Star Island, where the fishing was good, the living not bad, and the taxes and government imposition in general much reduced from the previous government of Massachusetts on Hog Island and Smuttynose.

THE ARRIVAL OF REV. JOHN TUCKE

Star Island became the home of most fishermen and their families by 1700; the town of Gosport, "God's port," was incorporated by the New Hampshire General Court soon after. The residents of *God's Port* believed that the presence, situation, and character of the islands were part of the will of God, and that without God's help, these islands and their inhabitants were forsaken. Even the most hardy and gruff fisherman sought stability and order, which required structures and institutions that promoted morality, prosperity, learning, and harmony. Gosport needed a permanent minister, and a good one at that—a man who possessed the right combination of sternness and patience; who could persevere yet accept the inevitable—and teach others to do the same; who humbled pride with piety; and who could help a town of potential ne'er-do-wells become a god-fearing, productive community. Such a man was the Reverend John Tucke, a Harvard educated pastor who ministered to the fishermen at Gosport, Star Island, from 1732 to 1773. Tucke had just the right qualities to become the moral, spiritual, intellectual, and social leader of the fishermen and fishwives of the Isles of Shoals during the eighteenth century.

John Tucke was born August 23, 1702, the firstborn to John and Bethiah Tucke. The father was a deacon in the congregational church, involved in local and provincial politics. The mother was from the Hobbs family of Hampton. Hampton was sixty-four years old in 1702, having been founded by religious pilgrims from Massachusetts who migrated north in 1638 to a land called Winnecunnet by the local natives. Winnecunnet was well situated on the trade routes paralleling the coast north and south. The new town of Hampton lacked the great harbors of some of its neighbors, such as Portsmouth to the north and Newburyport to the south. But the marshes were rich and grand, promising more than enough fodder to feed the town's livestock and generate surplus for trade.

Hampton, like most towns of seacoast New Hampshire, fell under the shadow of the Massachusetts Bay Puritans, who claimed a special covenant with God that gave them the right to implement His will over other, weaker neighbors. New England towns in 1700 considered religion the foundation for all other customs and institutions—government, diplomacy, human relations, thought, and trade. The power and influence of Massachusetts over the towns of New Hampshire was, therefore, irresistible. The "New England way" of identifying and implementing the will of God accommodated neither the religious alternatives of Catholics, Baptists, Anglicans, and Quakers, the temptations of a wealthy, material society, nor the influence of France, Spain, or any other country.

As he matured John Tucke learned the particulars of Hampton, where the air is tinged with salt, the winters are cold and furious, the salt marshes plentiful, the tide pools rank, and the sea ubiquitous. The Atlantic seacoast of New Hampshire provides plentiful opportunities to astonish the inquisitive child. The sea pounds the beaches, rolls in and out, rises and falls. All is endless movement. Shoals are hidden then revealed, then hidden again. Green water foams and crashes, manipulates all in its path. The child is easily hypnotized by the repetitive motion of the waves, the distant clouds lazy on the horizon, and the bright sun made brighter by the endless mirror of water. His moods flow in and out. His sense of time rises and falls with the tide. On the surface, all may appear peaceful enough. But below in the deep, leviathans of the mind lay in wait. When he least expects it, the strong undertow sucks him in, under the waves, where the cold, green water envelopes, overwhelms—and struggle is futile, as his will becomes the will of the sea.

John Tucke felt the call of God at Hampton. For such purpose he had been educated at Harvard, had studied to obtain his Master's degree, had served various seacoast parishes as an itinerant preacher, and had learned of the demands of Providence. At Hampton, Tucke met Mary Dole. Her dowry matched her beauty. Housekeeping was pleasant, and so was their love. Husband and wife had three children born to them at Hampton, two sons and a

Tucke family graves

daughter, each dying soon after birth. The death of the second, an infant daughter only three months old whose name is unrecorded, so affected Tucke that he declined a call from the parish at Chester, New Hampshire, to be their pastor, even though the citizens of Chester were willing to sustain their pastor's activities with an attractive salary. John and Mary went on, trying to create a family to rear and love. They were blessed with the birth of Benjamin in the spring of 1731. Tucke began to preach actively at several parishes, hoping for another call to labor for God. During the winter of 1731 he commuted to the Isles of Shoals, preaching to the fishermen, their wives and children. If any people needed love, hope, and redemption, it was the people of the Isles of Shoals. Tucke's piety and firmness impressed them, and they offered him a stable position as the pastor. All was set when a "very heavy Stroake of Providence" forced Tucke to delay. Benjamin, but a year old, died. The small headstone of his third born, next to those of his daughter and firstborn, John, reminded John Tucke of the eternal presence of God, directing, challenging, smiting, giving, and forgiving.

Eventually John Tucke made his way to the Isles of Shoals to make them his own, to minister to the island people, to raise his family and build his home, to live and to die. Just a few miles of sea separated Gosport and Hampton, yet to the Tucke family the two places seemed worlds apart.

Rev. Tucke baptized hundreds of children during his forty-one years at Gosport. On March 20, 1763, he baptized the newborn son of John and Sarah Newton. John was their first child, born to the couple two years after their marriage in 1747. The infant was baptized in December 1749 but died soon after. Having been absent from services and sacrament during the time of her travail, Sarah returned to the fold and renewed the covenant in November 1749, cleansing her of the "stain of sin" and re-establishing her relationship with God and fellow communicants. The "Records of the Church of Gosport," kept by Rev. Tucke during his tenure there, reveal scant information about most of the inhabitants. There are few details remaining from the lives of John and Sarah Newton. Besides John, the infant who died in 1749/1750, and their second child, also named John and born in 1763, the couple had Richard, baptized in 1753, Nanny, baptized in 1760, and James, their last, baptized in 1766. Sarah was forty-five years old when James was born; her husband John, perhaps older, died within a few years of James' birth. The widow Sarah Newton married widower Samuel Webber in 1771.

Whether or not John and Sarah Newton had a happy marriage is unclear. Sarah responded to the revival of religion, the Great Awakening, that occurred at Gosport as at so many American communities during the 1740s. There is, however, no evidence that her husband John ever owned the covenant with the Gosport community. Sarah was twenty-six at the time of her marriage. She was probably no great beauty, nor did she possess a large dowry. The couple appears to have spent their lives at Gosport, though there is a strange entry in the church records that Sarah "removed from hence" in August 1752. It is not clear if she moved with her husband, whose like removal Rev. Tucke did not record since he was not a communicant of the church, or whether Sarah moved because of marital trouble. Infidelity was all too common at the Isles of Shoals, and many mariners and their wives sought illusory solace for their anxiety and suffering in strong drink and sexual wantonness. At any rate, the couple lived at Gosport from 1753 until his death.

When the War of American Independence began in 1775, the presence of British frigates off the coast of New Hampshire, the disorder and privation of war, the disruption of the fishery, and the fear among the Patriot leaders that the British would use the islands as a Tory base led to most of the inhabitants fleeing to safe ports such as Portsmouth on the Piscataqua River and Newburyport on the Merrimack River. A few hardy, stubborn, and desperate people remained on Star Island to try to scrape out a living, though they had a reputation for degeneracy and poverty. Whether or not Sarah and her new husband Samuel Webber fled to the coast or stayed at Gosport is unknown. Hence the fate of Sarah's children is unclear. By this time Richard Newton would have been a man. But Nanny, John, and James were still young enough to be under mother's care. At the outbreak of the Revolution, John Newton was twelve. His father, then his stepfather, taught him the rudiments of fishing and seamanship.

JOHN NEWTON MEETS DUDLEY TYNG

The scant Gosport town and church records during the war lead one to suspect that John Newton remained at the Isles of Shoals. This is the implication of an obscure and incomplete manuscript penned by Dudley (Atkins) Tyng at some point after 1800. The manuscript, which can be found at the Massachusetts Historical Society, is a memoir of his experience with the Shoalers written at Newburyport, where Tyng was the Collector of Customs, a lawyer, and a community leader. "From early life the name of 'the Isles of

Shoals' had been familiar to me," Tyng recalled:

> ...as a place of resort for invalids, to whom the sea air
> had been recommended, and for parties of pleasure. I
> had known many of the inhabitants of the Islands,
> occasionnally [sic] visiting Newburyport for the
> procuring of salt and other necessaries for carrying on
> the Fisheries. Many of the children had been placed
> at service in families, or apprenticed to traders in
> Newburyport. In this way a frequent intercourse was
> maintained between the two places. It was here too
> that the inhabitants sought a market, as well for their
> *table fish*, which were almost exclusively cured on the
> Isles of Shoals, as for those other kinds suitable for the
> European and West India markets. In the sale of
> their Fish, these people found a rich reward of their
> enterprise and industry, being abundantly supplied
> with the comforts and conveniences of life. This state
> of things continued until the commencement of the
> revolutionary war. The exposed and defenceless [sic]
> situation of the islands caused the greater part of the
> inhabitants to remove to the main, leaving only a few
> families, who were probably too poor to meet the
> expense of such an emigration, or of too low a
> reputation to hope for a welcome in the well
> regulated societies on the main in their vicinity. From
> this time all civil order and all moral and religious
> instruction ceased; and the most deplorable
> ignorance, with vice in its most disgusting forms,
> overspread the settlement. In process of time some of
> the men, more shrewd and more industrious than the
> rest, began to improve their condition and to grow in
> some measure sensible of the degraded state of their
> society, and to wish for its amelioration.

One of these "shrewd" and "industrious" men was
John Newton, who by the 1790s owned his own fishing
boat, had learned to read and write, had emerged as a
leader of the small community at Gosport, and sought
moral and economic aid for the ailing community. Newton
felt a special affinity with Newburyport, perhaps because he
had spent some of the war years there, or because the
market for his fish was better than at Portsmouth.
Whatever the reason, Newton frequently rowed or sailed
his small boat into the harbor at Newburyport to trade, get

supplies, and renew his license to fish and trade at the customs office. As a resident of Star Island, which was adjoined to the state of New Hampshire, Newton should have registered at the customs office at Portsmouth. Dudley Tyng, who "in July 1795 . . . was appointed by President Washington to the office of collector of customs for the District of Newburyport," knew that Newton and other "owners of the few small fishing vessels then belonging to the Islands had considered themselves as attached to this district, and had been accustomed, though improperly to obtain their licenses here." Tyng, a great stickler for detail and typically inflexible in matters of business, felt sympathy for the poor fishermen and did not quibble about where they renewed their licenses.

When Dudley Tyng became Collector of Customs, Newburyport was a lively town of five thousand inhabitants. The tonnage of vessels carrying imports to and exports from the port grew dramatically during the 1790s, making it the busiest port north of Boston second only to Portsmouth on the Piscataqua River. The harbor is a well-protected cove on the Atlantic Ocean, formed at the mouth of the Merrimack River. An endless blue sea appears in the distance beyond the mass of billowing white sails. The fresh water of the Merrimack, which has completed its long journey that begins at the foothills of the White Mountains in New Hampshire, competes for dominance with the ocean brine of the rising tide. Salty air and fresh sea breezes cause one to pause and breathe deeply.

Dudley Tyng lived just a few blocks from the busy Custom House, where he spent his days registering and clearing the incoming goods of brigs and schooners, particularly molasses, cocoa, and coffee from the Caribbean, and the exports, such as fish and timber, of heavily-loaded ships bound for distant ports. Tyng rarely allowed anything to interrupt the business of the Custom House. Nevertheless one day of no particular significance in 1799, Tyng got to talking to the weather-beaten fisherman John Newton. The Shoaler Newton was not wont to complain, but when he realized he had the ear of the officious and articulate Tyng, he did not wait for a second chance. Newton told Tyng his own story of poverty and deprivation, how the revolutionary years of the 1770s changed Gosport from a prosperous, god-fearing fishing community to a god-forsaken rock lashed by the strong winds of time and sprayed by the cold waves of fortune. The exodus from the Isles of Shoals was never reversed. At the conclusion of the war most Shoalers lived impoverished lives on shore; they lacked the resources and the will to return to their former lives. Anyone who experiences calm harbors rarely wants to return to the lashing gales of the cold Atlantic. Gosport scarcely recovered during the 1780s and 1790s. The meetinghouse, the center and life of the community, was broken down physically and spiritually. The town lacked a minister, who for the Shoalers of the eighteenth century was also the censor, teacher, physician, and spiritual leader. A few of the stalwart, such as John Newton, served in town offices, such as they were. Since Newton was moderately prosperous and could read and write, it made sense that he serve as a selectman for the town. It was this role as a town leader that impelled Newton to end his tale of woe with a request that Dudley Tyng, an important man of affairs, use his position, connections, and benevolence to assist the Shoalers. Tyng agreed to help.

Tyng contacted the Society for the Propagation of the Gospel, which agreed to provide monetary and spiritual encouragement for a missionary to be sent to Gosport and for a new meetinghouse to be built to conduct religious services. Tyng had a chance to briefly meet the missionary, Rev. Jacob Emerson, when he stopped at Newburyport on his way to the Isles to begin his duties. A week later Tyng himself "procured a vessel" and set forth to the Isles of Shoals.

Small craft, the fishing shallop and the small ketch, regularly went back and forth the few miles from Newburyport to the Isles of Shoals. Assuming that there was no heavy fog on that September day, the eight isles appeared as they do today, small humps rising from the water. They are white, brown, and gray and appear irregular, neither shapely nor symmetrical. The captain of the boat upon which Dudley Tyng took passage would have navigated boats that lacked radar, diesel engines, and fiberglass hulls. No matter how often he had sailed these waters, the captain had to watch the helm carefully and order the dropping of the lead, measuring the depth of the water in fathoms, at regular intervals. The water was shallow and rocky about the isles, the wind was contrary, and the sea rough—better sailors had seen their last within sight of the Isles of Shoals. Captain, crew, and passengers observed, waited, and watched as the tiny craft skimmed the water toward Star Island and the town of Gosport.

Tyng stayed at Gosport for several days, during which time he acquired enough information on the history and state of affairs of the islands to pen, shortly after his visit, a long description, which was published in 1800. Tyng's informant was John Newton, who took the visitor on a tour of Star Island (and perhaps the others too), portraying its present condition and describing its recent past.

Tyng learned from Newton general information about the number, size, and physical characteristics of the islands. The "habitable" islands are "*Hog* Island, of about 350 acres; *Star* Island, of about 150 acres; *Haley's*, or *Smutty-Nose* Island, of about 100 acres." Five others are uninhabitable: "*Cedar*, *White*, *Londonners's*, *Malaga*, and *Duck Islands*; the largest of which contains about eight acres, the smallest one acre." The two men strolled about the islands that:

> have a dreary and inhospitable appearance, and but for their advantageous situation for carrying on the fisheries, would probably never have been inhabited. They are a bed of rocks, raising their disjointed heads above the water. The greater part of their surface is covered with a thick soil, yielding grass sufficient to support, during the summer and autumn, twenty or thirty cows, and about 150 sheep. The sheep raised here are usually killed before winter. Nearly half the sward, on Star Island, has, within a few years, been cut up by the necessitous inhabitants, dried and burnt, instead of more solid fuel. Upon all the islands there are chasms in the rocks, several yards wide, and from one to ten deep, occasioned, if we may judge from appearances, by some violent earthquake. In some places, acres of rock are broken off from the rest of the island; and through the cracks or guts, the water, at high tides and in storms, rushes in torrents.

Tyng learned that Newton and other inhabitants of Star Island gathered rain water for drinking and cooking; only

Hog Island had a "perennial spring." Few trees grew on the islands, and soil for gardens was scarce. The inhabitants relied on fish for their food as well as their occupation. The fishing was still good. Newton informed his visitor that "winter or dumb fish" is a "fairer, larger, and thicker fish" than those caught during summer. "The dumb fish is consumed chiefly in New-England, and is considered, by connoisseurs in fish, the best in the world." Notwithstanding that dumb fish "command a higher price" and the Isles of Shoals "have the preference in [the] market" for fish, the inhabitants remained miserably poor, living in "loathsome" homes. They were generally ignorant, "dirty, and wicked," and heavily dependent upon "ardent spirits." Their lives were clearly very difficult. Dumb fish was the basis of their livelihood, yet it must be caught in winter, and "the hardships endured in taking the winter fish are inconceivable by all but eye witnesses." Nevertheless the Isles of Shoals had a tradition of being a place for health. Although "the inhabitants are not remarkable for longevity," Tyng believed that the climate "at all seasons" is "very healthful." Newton told Tyng that the Rev. Tucke "used to say, that, in the winter season, the weather at the Shoals was 'a thin under waistcoat warmer, than in the same parallel of latitude on the main.'"

The Rev. John Tucke was a "good man" who, when he died in 1773, was "deeply and universally lamented," according to John Newton and others still living on the Isles who remembered him. One declared that Tucke and his wife Mary, who predeceased him by only two months, "were lovely and pleasant in their lives, and in their deaths they were not divided." Rev. Tucke was severely missed. The twenty-six years since his death had seen a declining disposition among the Shoalers "to support the ordinances of religion." Children's spiritual needs were neglected, and parents provided "no regular school for the education of their children."

The inhabitants, like the children of Israel of old, took to "the vices of cursing and swearing, drunkenness, quarrelling, and disobedience to parents." Before Tucke's death the Shoalers were thriving and prosperous, the people god-fearing, and the society of the islands sufficiently sophisticated so "that gentlemen, from some of the principal towns on the

Gosport Chapel, Star Island, 1800s

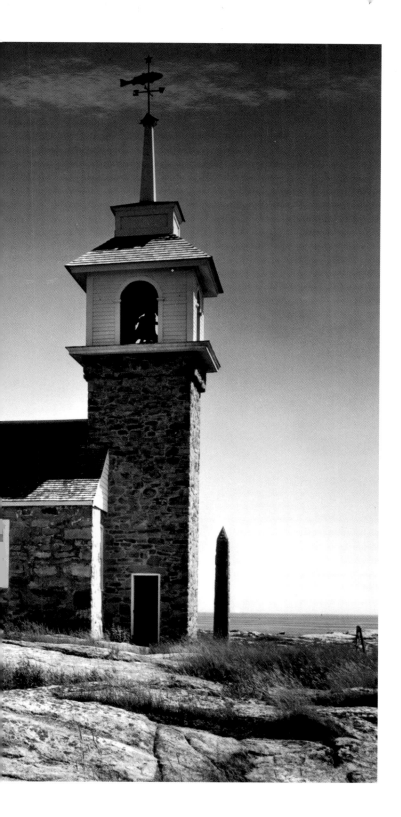

Star Island

A delightful day trip involves taking one of the many cruise ships that sails out of Portsmouth Harbor and Rye Harbor to Star Island at the Isles of Shoals. Besides the modern conference center, the visitor can see the granite monument to Captain John Smith and view the old Gosport parish church where the likes of the Rev. John Tucke once held sway. Best of all is to take in the sea air, to be invigorated as Nathaniel Hawthorne once was, to explore the tiny island and imagine oneself a fisherman or fishwife from three hundred years ago.

sea coast, sent their sons here for literary instruction."

Tyng heard from the inhabitants that Rev. Tucke was "of humble and unaffected piety, of diligence and fidelity in the service of the ministry." Tucke was, according to one Shoaler, "given to hospitality, and apt to teach." He was a "physician of body and of soul" who "went about doing good among all classes of the people of his charge, and his labours were not in vain in the Lord. Under his nurturing, pastoral care; his people increased in numbers and in wealth, in knowledge, piety and respectability."

Hawthorne on Vacation

Certainly, the Rev. John Tucke of the Isles of Shoals was an exceptional man, a fisher of men, one who made his mark among thousands of men and women but in a quiet, anonymous way, without fanfare, seeking the simple reward of service to others in love. The love of the Shoalers toward this man remained for a generation after his death. Dudley Tyng witnessed the ongoing affection extended toward a man long dead. Another visitor to the Shoals fifty years later also heard of the remarkable influence of John Tucke. This man, the writer Nathaniel Hawthorne, was similarly attracted to the past of the Isles of Shoals. During a period of several weeks, in the late summer of 1852, Hawthorne strolled about Star Island, looking at the remains of Gosport, seeking information of what once was. Eventually he turned to the documents of the past, the manuscripts that survived from colonial Gosport, believing that the records of the past held insights into the present.

Nathaniel Hawthorne came to the Isles of Shoals for a long needed vacation after having helped his friend Franklin

Pierce campaign for the presidency of the United States; Hawthorne had just finished a biography of Pierce that would in the end help propel Pierce to the highest office. Pierce had promised Hawthorne that the two friends would rendezvous at the Isles for a brief respite from politics.

Franklin Pierce hailed from Hillsboro, New Hampshire. He was a lawyer and a past New Hampshire representative to the U. S. House and Senate. Pierce was an unusual candidate for president as a Democrat, historically a pro-slave party, from New Hampshire, a state without slaves. But Pierce believed that slavery was a non-issue in 1852 and appeared as a compromise candidate to hold the Democrats, as well as the nation, together. Pierce had just garnered the nomination of the Democratic party for president of the United States.

By the time Franklin Pierce arrived at the Isles of Shoals, Hawthorne had been there for three days. Already he had grown used to the invitation to indolence and relaxation that the Shoals offered the visitor. Hawthorne happily complied to the marine environment, the ceaseless sound—at times but a murmur—of the sea, the cool breezes, the call of gulls, as well as the absence of order and regularity in a person's daily itinerary and among the islands themselves. He stayed at Appledore (Hog) Island at the hotel owned by Thomas Laighton; he quickly became friends with a would-be actor, Levi Thaxter, and his beautiful young wife Celia, daughter of Thomas Laighton. When Hawthorne met her she was but seventeen years old. Already she was a charming hostess, well read, and a wonderful singer. She was dearly attached to the Isles of Shoals. As the years passed she wrote narratives and poems to express her love for the islands and their past. Twenty years after Hawthorne's visit, she wrote *Among the Isles of Shoals*, a narrative account of her experiences at the Isles.

Upon the arrival of Franklin Pierce on September 6, the men rowed over to Star Island to inspect the remains of the town of Gosport. [Hawthorne wrote about this and other wanderings about the Isles in a journal that would eventually become the *American Notebooks*.] They discovered Rev. John Tucke's grave and got from the alcoholic town clerk the old records of the town. Hawthorne remarked that the records, "commencing in

Celia, John, and Karl Thaxter, 1856

Celia Laighton Thaxter (1835–1894)

New Hampshire writer and poet Celia Thaxter was born in Portsmouth to Thomas and Eliza Laighton. Her father moved the family to the Isles of Shoals in 1839, where Celia spent her youth and old age. She married Levi Thatcher in 1851 and graced Appledore Island where her father owned Appledore House, a summer hotel visited by the likes of Nathaniel Hawthorne and Mark Twain. After her marriage and relocation to Massachusetts, Celia began writing poetry in the 1850s in part to dispel her constant longing for the Isles of Shoals. In 1873 she published *Among the Isles of Shoals* and followed this with other collections. Her poems capture the beauty and privation of life on these barren rocks jutting from the sea, and she is best known for the following work:

Sandpiper

Across the narrow beach we flit,
One little sandpiper and I,
And fast I gather, bit by bit,
The scattered drift-wood bleached and dry.
The wild waves reach their hands for it,
The wild wind raves, the tide runs high,
As up and down the beach we flit,
One little sandpiper and I.
Above our heads the sullen clouds
Scud black and swift across the sky:
Like silent ghosts in misty shrouds
Stand out the white light-houses high.
Almost as far as eye can reach
I see the close-reefed vessels fly,
As fast we flit along the beach,
One little sandpiper and I.
I watch him as he skims along,
Uttering his sweet and mournful cry;
He starts not at my fitful song,
Or flash of fluttering drapery.
He has no thought of any wrong;
He scans me with a fearless eye;
Staunch friends are we, well tried and strong,
The little sandpiper and I.
Comrade, where wilt thou be to-night,
When the loosed storm breaks furiously?
My drift-wood fire will burn so bright!
To what warm shelter canst thou fly?
I do not fear for thee, though wroth
The tempest rushes through the sky;
For are we not God's children both,
Thou, little sandpiper, and I?

—*Stories and Poems for Children (1895)*

1732," are "in a beautiful style of penmanship." The records were written in John Tucke's hand. Hawthorne, fascinated by the records and always on the lookout for vignettes and tidbits from New England's past that might provide fodder for fiction, recorded plentiful excerpts. Church records, of course, can be rather banal. But Hawthorne found much to interest him. The Shoalers of the eighteenth century broke all too often the seventh commandment against adultery. Tucke required confession of the sin in front of the entire parish before the sinner was received back into the fold for communion. Another sin was celebrating Christmas, a holiday with supposed pagan origins. Many parishioners drank too much rum not only on Christmas day but every other day of the year. At one point Rev. Tucke made a complete list of the sins found at Gosport, of which from the church records the following is only a portion:

> [Y]e making light of Eternal Destruction and Damnation; ye earthly and sensual mindedness; ye stupidity under God's judgments; ye contention in families and among neighbors; ye Drunkenness and uncleanness; ye Talebearing, Backbiting, Lying & Stealing; ye Deceit, Over-reaching, & Defrauding of Persons of their just due;—these being but some of the many & crying sins among us.

Such continual reminders of sinful behavior elicited from the inhabitants of Gosport not disgust and hatred but rather love and respect. Long after Tucke's death in 1773, the Shoalers remembered him. In 1914 the people of New Hampshire made concrete the esteem they continued to feel toward Tucke by erecting a monument, a stone obelisk, in his honor.

Hawthorne, Pierce, and party, led by their drunken guide, "dressed in the ordinary fisherman's style, red baize shirt, trowsers tucked into large boots," strolled about the island. The guide pointed out remarkable sights such as "Betty Moody's Hole," where a hapless colonial dame hid from attacking Native Americans long ago before the American Revolution. At another singular spot, a rocky outcrop jutting out toward the sea, "a young woman residing at Gosport, in the capacity of school-teacher," who "was of a romantic turn, and used to go and sit on this point of rock, to view the waves," one day was swept by the waves into the sea. This horrible event happened in 1848, and the spot came to be known as "Miss Underhill's Chair." Another place, "near the centre of the island," a huge monolith "about breast-high," had in the distant past apparently emerged from its rocky depths. Hawthorne commented it was "incalculably aged"; the local inhabitants believed it emerged on the day of Christ's crucifixion. There were, of course, stories of other past events, such as the visit of pirates to the Isles—prospecting for buried pirate treasure was a frequent occupation of the Isles of Shoals. Also frequent was the use of a make-shift "bowling-alley, . . . at which some of the young fishermen were rolling."

On September 9, Pierce and companions having departed, Thaxter and Hawthorne visited White Island, the southernmost of the Isles of Shoals, which hosted the lighthouse. The two men climbed the ladder to the top of the cylindrical structure, where was the "lanthern, . . . a revolving light, with several great illuminators of copper silvered, and colored lamp glasses." The lighthouse keeper was twice a widower and an alcoholic; Hawthorne thought he had "a sneaking kind of look." But of course anyone who lived year-round on such a lonely rock in the sea would inevitably have such a look. The author of *The House of Seven Gables* saw much that was mysterious in life, and his credulous mind had much upon which to ruminate during his sojourn to the islands. Mr. and Mrs. Thaxter, for example, told him of an apparent ghost that had visited their home one day not too long ago. She was an old woman who came in uninvited and warmed her feet by the fire before vanishing. The islanders were loath to walk about the islands at night for fear of running into Old Bob, "who was one of Captain Kidd's men, and was slain for the protection of the [pirate] treasure." Old Bob appeared often enough that Hawthorne gathered a complete description: He "has a ring round his neck; and is supposed either to have been hung, or to have had his throat cut; but he steadfastly declines telling the mode of his death. There is a luminous appearance about him, as he walks. His face is pale, and very dreadful."

At one point during his solitary wanderings about the Isles of Shoals, Nathaniel Hawthorne happened by "a cairn, a mere heap of stones, thrown together as they came to hand." The cairn was "seven feet high, and probably ten or twelve in diameter at its base." Thomas Laighton informed Hawthorne that this was an ancient monument to Captain John Smith, the first known visitor to the Isles from across the Atlantic. In time others would find such an inelegant memorial to be insufficient, buiding a proper monument in 1914 to commemorate Smith's sojourn to the Isles.

At the southern extreme of Star Island, a promontory that juts into the Atlantic Ocean and bars the wind and waves, stands a solitary, weather-beaten monument to exploration and discovery and to the beginnings of New Hampshire. The monument is a seamark that records the brief entrance and exit of Captain John Smith into the history of New England. It was Smith, the author of *A Description of New England* (1616), who more than any other explorer opened up New Hampshire and New England to settlement. From the vantage point of Smith's monument one can see, on a clear day, the New Hampshire shoreline stretching north to south, from the mouth of the Piscataqua River to near the mouth of the Merrimack River. The Piscataqua and Merrimack beckoned early explorers to sail up their broad paths past inviting harbors into the interior, beyond the fall line to the deep forests of pine and birch. From the Isles of Shoals one can sometimes see the distant peak of Mount Washington, which was the ultimate goal of many explorers who began their journey from the sea, into the rivers, and beyond.

2

THE PISCATAQUA VALLEY

The Route 66 of the East coast is Route 1, traversing America from Florida to northern Maine. Route 1 covers but a short distance in New Hampshire, but that is a busy, crowded, historical journey. Travelers for 400 years have wandered, marched, ridden, and driven Route 1 and its earlier manifestations. George Washington entered New Hampshire on this famous road when in 1789 he made his tour of northern states. The route follows the same path today as then, over 200 years ago. Washington on his journey saw farms, small towns, meetinghouses, and taverns. Today's motorist sees much of the same, now crowded amid gas stations, antique shops, fish-markets, restaurants, and much more.

THE VIEW FROM ROUTE 1

Route 1 enters New Hampshire from the south at Seabrook, famous for its greyhound racing and New Hampshire's only nuclear power plant, which appears ominously yet majestically amid miles of salt marshes. From Seabrook the traveler enters Hampton Falls, settled in 1640, a beautiful old town with the green and parade ground suitably hosting the cannon that recall past wars. After crossing marshland—the rank smell of decaying seaweed mixing with fresh salt air and the extensive horizon in all directions, a unique and unexpected sight in such a forested state—one arrives at Hampton.

The tall marsh grasses of Hampton was what originally attracted the Rev. Stephen Batchellor and other immigrants from Massachusetts when they arrived at the site of the Native American village of Winnacunnet in 1638. Batchellor led farmers who drove their cattle to be fatted by grazing on the rich grass. They were a simple people, Puritans who believed that God directed their move to New Hampshire and willed that they continue to be subject to the Puritan colony of Massachusetts Bay, headquartered in Boston.

Hampton was then one of four early settlements in New Hampshire, the other three being Exeter on the Squamscott River, Dover on the Cocheco River, and Portsmouth on the Piscataqua River. Exeter like Hampton was settled in 1638 by Puritans journeying north from Massachusetts. The Rev. John Wheelwright, a brother of the Puritan firebrand Anne Hutchinson, led his followers to the rich marshland at the western end of the Great Bay, an island estuary of mingling fresh and sea water around which many of the early towns of New Hampshire were built. Newington, on the southern edge of Great Bay and originally part of Portsmouth, was founded as a distinct parish in 1712. Newmarket on the Lamprey River, a shipbuilding and later mill center, was settled in the 1640s and incorporated in 1727. Durham, originally called Oyster River and now the site of the University of New Hampshire, was settled in the late 1600s. Dover was one of the earliest settlements in New Hampshire (1633), originally an extension of a fishing operation begun by Edward Hilton. East of Dover is Portsmouth, originally called Strawbery Banke, the site of the first English exploration in 1603. Portsmouth is at the northern limit of Route 1 in New Hampshire. Between Portsmouth and Hampton are several picturesque towns. North Hampton was incorporated in 1742 though settled a century before. Rye was originally a part of Portsmouth, once called Sandy Beach. And the inland town of Greenland appears as it once did two hundred years ago, part of the anachronistic flavor of New Hampshire that makes exploring the state by automobile exhilarating.

At Hampton, Route 1 diverges to an arm, Route 1A, that takes the slow, oceanic route along the coast. Route 1A provides the extremes of coastal New Hampshire. Traveling from south to north, 1A takes the motorist through Hampton Beach, a resort area for over 100 years. The long, wide beach is what originally brought tourists to Hampton Beach in the late nineteenth century. Today it is overcrowded and gaudy, the delight of the hedonist and exhibitionist, a place of bars, casinos, shops, thousands of partially clad sun-worshipers, and an endless stream of autos and motorcycles. The easterly breezes that skim the always cool waters of the New Hampshire coastline refreshes the summer crowds, but during the long winter they also make Hampton Beach empty, a place of summer memories.

The New Hampshire coast is only 18 miles long, forming part of a great arc that extends from Cape Elizabeth in Maine to Cape Ann in Massachusetts. In fact a visitor can sometimes spy Cape Ann from New Hampshire beaches, as well as Plum Island at the mouth of the Merrimack River. Two small headlands at Hampton Beach are Big Boars Head and Little Boars Head. Upon reaching the former, the traveler begins to see what will remain a constant visual companion as he continues his journey north on Route 1A: the Isles of Shoals. Except on rainy and foggy days, the Isles provide a beautiful, romantic vision for the landlubber. On clear days they seem to float on the surface, just out of reach, the white buildings, lighthouse, and Tucke monument plainly visible. Cruise ships make daily runs to and from the Isles, even in winter. The *Thomas Laighton* is often seen by the beachcomber on her journey from the Piscataqua to the Isles. Competing for attention are numerous fishing and lobster boats making their daily rounds. Sailing vessels appear distantly on the horizon. Sometimes a large freighter shipping out from Portsmouth harbor lumbers past the Isles of Shoals.

The drive along Route 1A from North Beach around Little Boars Head to North Hampton and Jenness beaches features a delightful winding path in which the explorer is hemmed by an alternating rocky and sandy coast to the east and marshland and large graceful mansions to the west. Sunday mornings, residents and tourists alike join together at St. Andrews Episcopal Church, by the sea. St. Andrews, open only for Eucharist and morning prayer during summer months when salt air invigorates morning gatherings, features an archaic, Tudor stone building, a church bell in a central cupola, a lawn surrounded by trees, an old stone wall weathered by many dozens of years, and graves and headstones of past parishioners. Old photographs of over a century ago, soon after the church was built in 1876, show that it has hardly changed in 128 years.

Rye, an old town once a part of Portsmouth, was in the 1800s a prime tourist attraction and summer resort.

President Franklin Pierce of New Hampshire owned a cottage at Little Boars Head, where he entertained notables such as his friend Nathaniel Hawthorne. Large graceful hotels, such as the Farragut and the Atlantic House, entertained other statesmen and writers over the years. It was just a short walk from the Farragut to St. Andrews. Frank Philbrick, whose family owned the Farragut, donated the land for St. Andrews. The building of the church was largely due to the financial support of Edward Abbot, whose company built the Concord Coach.

There are very few harbors along New Hampshire's shoal and sand ridden coast. One exception is Rye Harbor,

Merrimack River Rattlesnake Hill granite quarry. Engraving circa 1830s

where fishing boats, lobster boats, pleasure craft, and cruise
ships have docked for well over a century. Rye Harbor was
well known to mariners who sailed the east coast north and
south and who might have experienced heavy seas
requiring a safe haven. Some boats during the age of sail
could not negotiate the shoal waters and gales off Concord
Point in Rye: the *Victor* sank in 1882, as did the *Lizzie Carr*
in 1905. The latter schooner cracked up near Wallis Sands
State Park. Only recently archeologists from Plymouth
State University (in Plymouth, New Hampshire) have

excavated some of the ruins of the *Lizzie Carr*, buried for almost a century by Wallis Beach sand.

The last point on the New Hampshire coast to which Route 1A takes the traveler is Odiorne Point, a rocky pincer that juts into the sea. The peninsula from Odiorne Point to Little Harbor hosted one of the first settlements in the early 1600s. David Thomson, who was employed by the English proprietors of New Hampshire, Ferdinando Gorges and John Mason, crossed the Atlantic in 1621 to this beautiful spot at the mouth of the Piscataqua River. King James I granted proprietary rights to Gorges and Mason to settle the Piscataqua Valley and hinterland. The proprietors sent many agents to the region, dubbed New Hampshire by Mason, in the 1620s and 1630s to establish fishing camps, to begin exploiting the inland fur and timber resources, and to befriend (or intimidate) local Native American tribes. These first English settlers, such as Walter Neal, Edward Hilton, Darby Field, Ambrose Gibbins, and David Thomson, got along well with the few Algonquian tribes that maintained a sparse presence in the region. Legend has it that the chiefs, or sachems, of such tribes as the Penacook sold land to the English. Records of land deals between sachems such as Passaconaway and English negotiators have been generally branded as illegitimate by scholars. The material point was that by 1650 the English took control of the seacoast, the Piscataqua Valley, and inland waterways and began to build viable communities, the most significant being Portsmouth.

Odiorne Point State Park today features walking trails that take the pedestrian back into the human and natural past. Waves wash upon the massive granite rocks of the point. Seaweed and beach peas lace themselves among the interstices of the rocks. Some boulders are covered in the slimy green sea flora. Countless barnacles and snails inhabit other rocks. The remnants of lobster traps mingle with driftwood. The smell of the sea mingles with the cries of gulls soaring high overhead. A nature center provides concrete data to supplement the subjective experience of the park.

From Odiorne, 1A takes the motorist to Portsmouth by way of Sagamore Creek. At one point along the drive the road offers a diversion to the right, turning onto which the motorist makes his way down a narrow lane to the onetime

Thomas Bailey Aldrich, 1836–1907

Thomas Bailey Aldrich wrote books on his experience living for a few years as a youth at Portsmouth. His *The Story of a Bad Boy* recalls these years from 1849–1852, when he lived with his grandparents in a white clapboard house with black shutters on Court Street in Portsmouth. This house is currently part of the Strawbery Banke Museum. Near the end of his life Aldrich returned to Portsmouth to pen *An Old Town by the Sea*. The book opens with the following poem:

Piscataqua River

Thou singest by the gleaming isles,
By woods, and fields of corn,
Thou singest, and the sunlight smiles
Upon my birthday morn.

But I within a city, I,
So full of vague unrest,
Would almost give my life to lie
An hour upon thy breast!

To let the wherry listless go,
And, wrapt in dreamy joy,
Dip, and surge idly to and fro,
Like the red harbor-buoy;

To sit in happy indolence,
To rest upon the oars,
And catch the heavy earthy scents
That blow from summer shores;

To see the rounded sun go down,
And with its parting fires
Light up the windows of the town
And burn the tapering spires;

And then to hear the muffled tolls
From steeples slim and white,

And watch, among the Isles of Shoals,
The Beacon's orange light.

O River! flowing to the main
Through woods, and fields of corn,
Hear thou my longing and my pain
This sunny birthday morn;

And take this song which fancy shapes
To music like thine own,
And sing it to the cliffs and capes
And crags where I am known!

Prescott Park, Portsmouth

Prescott Park is devoted to history, culture, and gardens. It sits between Strawbery Banke Museum and Portsmouth Harbor. At the east end of the park is the Point of Graves, a beautiful if solemn cemetery dating to the 1600s. Also at Prescott Park is the Sheafe Warehouse, dating back to 1700, as well as a restoration of an early gundalow, which sits at its moorings awaiting the visitor's inspection. Prescott Park features outdoor plays in the summer and a wonderful flower garden. Also at the park is the Liberty Pole, which was raised by rebellious colonials in 1765 in opposition to the Stamp Act.

estate of Benning Wentworth, Governor of New Hamp-shire from 1741 to 1767. Wentworth was one of the most fascinating of New Hampshire's colonial governors, bringing a certain elegance to the position but overly (and overtly) concerned with acquiring personal wealth at the expense of good government. His mansion was and is a beautiful location with which to look out upon the Piscataqua River and dream of days long past.

Another diversion to Portsmouth is Route 1B, which brings the traveler through the delightful center of Newcastle, where the houses, cemeteries, and meetinghouse look like the New England town of the imagination. The congregational church of the first parish, organized in 1653, is a proper two-story structure, the clapboard exterior painted white complimented appropriately by black shutters. In the eighteenth century, church pews were wooden, uncomfortable, set row by row, originally according to the rank and wealth of the parishioners. Town leaders maintained the pews nearest the pulpit. Ne'er-do-wells, the poor, people of color, orphans, and the homeless stood in the rear or watched from the balcony. Some of the members of these great if immodest Newcastle families lie buried across the street, forever in the shadow of the church.

Also known as Great Island, Newcastle is a picturesque town on a large island that lies at the mouth of the Piscataqua River. Great Island was the center, along with the Isles of Shoals, of the seventeenth-century New Hampshire fishing comm-unity. The island was of strategic value not only economically but politically, and the first settlers of the Piscataqua took due care to secure it with a series of forts. As a result, during colonial times Great Island was sometimes known as Castle Island. After 1700, the fort was named for King William and Queen Mary. Fort William and Mary protected Portsmouth harbor during the many wars fought between the English and French, especially the last, most significant conflict, the French-Indian War (1755-1763). After 1763, however, as conflict emerged between the American colonists and the British Crown, Fort William and Mary became a focal point of American resistance. In 1774 the fort was taken by colonial rebels led by John Langdon and John Sullivan, who would each play important roles in the subsequent War of American Independence. After the successful

Fort Constitution, Newcastle

Fort Constitution at the mouth of the Piscataqua River has had an imposing presence in New Hampshire for almost four hundred years. The fort played an active role in the defense of Portsmouth Harbor through many wars, the last being World War II. Today the remains of Fort Constitution are located on United States government land adjacent to a U. S. Coast Guard station. The traveler reaches it on Route 1B in Newcastle. The New Hampshire Division of Parks and Recreation maintains the fort, which allows the visitor to stroll its grounds, examining the old granite walls, magazines for ammunition such as black powder, rows of pintles to position lethal artillery, look-out points, and gun turrets for massive cannon that pointed toward the entrance of the harbor, where enemy ships approached from the sea. A lighthouse warns the many passing pleasure craft, fishing boats, tankers, and tall ships to beware this rocky outcrop on Great Island.

conclusion of the war and the inauguration of the new government under the Constitution, Fort William and Mary was renamed Fort Constitution. The fort had a continuing role in subsequent conflicts, such as the War of 1812. Many of the huge granite blocks that comprise the walls date from just before the War of 1812, a renewed conflict with the mighty British Empire and its dangerous fleet of military frigates. Fort Constitution protected Portsmouth harbor during the Spanish-American War as

well as during World War II. The town continues to host a World War II lookout tower.

Route 1B returns to Portsmouth, once again entering into the past. Near the harbor on Hunking Lane and Marcy Street are well-maintained clapboard homes, brightly painted in pastels, shutters ready to be closed to lock out the cold salt air of winter. The lanes are winding and narrow, as is the past of this town. Initially called Strawbery Banke, Portsmouth has been the most important port north of Boston for close to 400 years. Situated near the mouth of the Piscataqua River, Portsmouth features secure, deep

Portsmouth Naval Shipyard, circa WWI

harbors, dozens of historical landmarks, the still operating Portsmouth Naval Shipyard, and perhaps the highlight of historical Portsmouth, Strawbery Banke Museum.

Strawbery Banke was the site of one of the earliest settlements in New Hampshire. Martin Pring sailed up the Piscataqua River in 1603 and perhaps strolled among the strawberry bushes on the southern shore of the river. Here he found good moorings for his ships. By the 1620s agents of Ferdinando Gorges and Captain John Mason, proprietors of the Laconia Company, built a Great House at Strawbery Banke. Settlers engaged in the fishing industry, and lived a footloose life. During the 1640s, with Gorges and Mason dead and a bustling village emerging at Strawbery Banke, the villagers requested that the colony of Massachusetts Bay to the south incorporate Strawbery Banke into their jurisdiction and protection. The inhabitants also requested that the General Court grant a change of name. Strawbery Banke became Portsmouth, which would quickly emerge as the most important seaport of northern New England.

Puddle Dock, the small inlet that formed the core of Strawbery Banke, became the cultural and economic center of colonial Portsmouth. At Puddle Dock merchants built their saltbox homes and federal-style mansions and constructed wooden wharves to the inlet where small barks and gundalows—single-masted flat-bottomed cargo carriers—were moored to receive or dispose of lumber, fish, salt, and other trade goods. Near here Captain John Paul Jones awaited the outfitting of the *Providence* in 1777. John Langdon, revolutionary signer of the Declaration of Independence and President of the State of New Hampshire, paced the lanes of Strawbery Banke awaiting news of his merchant vessels. Up the road from Puddle Dock was the South Parish, where Nathaniel Rogers preached and Captain John Pickering provided secular leadership. Pickering donated land for use as a town cemetery: the Point of Graves is just east of Strawbery Banke adjacent to Prescott Park. Wandering north to the center of Portsmouth, one comes to Market Square, dominated by the spire of the North Parish. Rev. Joseph Buckminster once stood at the pulpit. Continuing in this tour of the anachronistic streets of Portsmouth, the pedestrian comes to St. John's Episcopal Church, originally called Queen's Chapel, where such men as Benning Wentworth, the New Hampshire colonial governor, rest in the Wentworth family tomb.

Portsmouth harbor has for three centuries held an important strategic position for American shipping and military actions. Before 1800, the shipyards of Portsmouth harbor built and repaired some of the most important ships of the American Navy, including the *Providence*, Captain John

Paul Jones's ship, the *America*, given to France at the end of the Revolutionary War, and "Old Ironsides," the *U.S.S. Constitution*. The latter ship was not built, but rather repaired at the Portsmouth Naval Shipyard, inaugurated by the U. S. government in 1800. The shipyard over the years has constructed and repaired clipper ships, ironclads (used first in the Civil War), the massive steel transport ships of World War I, and sub-marines, including, after World War II, nuclear subs.

THE PISCATAQUA VALLEY ALGONQUIANS

The east wind blowing up the Piscataqua Valley over these waters once, over four hundred years ago in 1603, brought English sailor Martin Pring to explore the shores of the Piscataqua. Living here and elsewhere along the coast and rivers of New Hampshire were various Native American tribes, most of whom spoke the Algonquin tongue. They were an agricultural people, having for thousands of years practiced simple farming techniques, yet with mixed

Blue Job Mountain

One of the best ways to see New Hampshire is to climb a mountain on a clear day. There are of course scores of 3000-foot, 4000-foot, and 5000-foot mountains, not to mention Mount Washington at over 6000 feet. By comparison Blue Job Mountain in Strafford County, standing at 1356 feet, is small indeed. This peak stands somewhat alone among hilly, forested land in eastern New Hampshire. From its rocky, tree-lined slope, Big River and Berry's River descend to Suncook River and Bellamy River, respectively. Atop Blue Job is a fire tower periodically manned by a ranger to watch for fires forming in the surrounding forest. From the tower on a clear day, the sightseer can make out the landscape of New Hampshire, hills and valleys, rivers and ponds. In the distance north are the Presidentials, highlighted by Mount Washington. East is the Atlantic. Distant landmarks of surrounding towns might be seen as well. The joy of Blue Job is not in the mountains nor the vista that opens before the observer. Rather, the short forty-five minute climb brings the reward (in summer) of a host of blueberry bushes, ripe and juicy. Many an explorer has climbed the stair-like stony steps of Blue Job to enjoy its spectacular repast.

success. As a result they were also forced to hunt, sometimes roaming through the dense north woods in the winter foraging for food. In late winter they cut the maple tree and collected the sap, boiling it into a thick syrup or a fine sugar. They cleared the land for planting by means of girdling trees—making lethal incisions at the base of the trunk and waiting for it to die and crumble—and by burning underbrush and open land. The Algonquians used stone, bone, and wooden tools, fashioning axes, adzes, knives, chisels, mortars, awls, needles, and the like through a painstaking methods of grinding, polishing, cutting, chipping, and so on. They often practiced trade, but too often war as well, which helped to divide and isolate different tribes, and kept the population from advancing too far.

The material culture of the Algonquians was sophisticated according to the limited technological resources available to them. They fashioned stone pots, wooden utensils, and baskets of all shapes and sizes. Their wigwams, often made of the white (paper) birch tree, were snug and functional. Their canoes, also made from the paper birch, were light, buoyant, and sturdy. Clothing was made of leather. Women wore their hair in long braided plaits; men cut their hair but left a scalp lock in the back of the head or a "Mohawk" running along the middle back to front. They used wampum, made of shells, for trade and the calumet (or peace pipe) in religious and diplomatic ceremonies. Shamans served as religious leaders, and spiritual and physical healers. All of the New England tribes were animists and pantheists who believed in a universal Great Spirit.

The Algonquin tribes of New Hampshire like those of Maine generally tolerated the arrival of the English, and often bargained away their lands to maintain harmony. Overwhelmed more by population and disease than warfare, remnants of the great tribes of the past retreated further into the hinterland, following rivers and streams north and west. The great chief of the Penacook tribe of the Merrimack Valley, Passaconaway, tried to maintain the dignity of his power and Penacook independence. Yet it was a futile task in which he was engaged. According to legend when he died his angry spirit ascended Mount Washington to rumble and storm and haunt forever. His son Wonnalancet and grandnephew Kancamangus also retreated north, as did so many other nameless people from the varied, mostly forgotten tribes of the seacoast.

The Algonquin tribes typically got along better with the French than the English. The French were more willing to learn from and respect Indian culture, and sought to convert them to Catholicism in a loving, if patronizing, fashion. The Indians returned the French concern by allying with them against the English in various wars of the seventeenth and eighteenth centuries. The Algonquin tribes assisted the French in King William's War (1689–1697), Queen Anne's War (1703–1713), Dummer's War (1722–1725), King George's War (1744–1749), and the French-Indian War (1755–1763). By and large she Algonquins successfully terrorized the settlers, capturing some and bringing them to New France. Both sides committed atrocities against the other: burning, scalping, torturing, murdering. These wars were chronicled by Jeremy Belknap in his *History of New-Hampshire*, and before him by the Portsmouth resident Samuel Penhallow in *The History of the Wars of New-England with the Eastern Indians*. By the time Penhallow wrote his book at Portsmouth in 1726 the Native American presence along the Piscataqua was negligible.

THE TRIP TO DOVER

St. John's Episcopal Church sits atop a small eminence next to Portsmouth harbor, from which the observer may look west to the broad Piscataqua on its winding descent from Dover Point. English mariners 400 years ago crawled up the narrow, maze-like Piscataqua, their three-masted ships dependent upon the east wind to carry them through the contrary current of the Piscataqua River. Local Algonquian tribes had an easier time in their birch-bark canoes, light and swift. Whether one ascends by the cumbersome pinnace, the bark canoe, the modern yacht, or diesel powered boat, the Piscataqua leads one upriver to its confluence with several rivers and the Little Bay and Great Bay. The motorist reaches the same point taking Route 4 north toward Dover and Durham. Crossing the Piscataqua by bridge at Dover (Hilton) Point, one may get off the highway to rest at Hilton Park, named for the early settler Edward Hilton, who established a fishing center in 1623 at this point that juts into merging waters. The strait between Dover Point and Newington, called Bloody Point in the colonial period, was crossed by ferry as early as 1640.

Corporation House, Dover, circa 1830

Newington, originally a part of Portsmouth, separated to form an independent parish in the early years of the eighteenth century. The Congregational church, which still stands, was built in 1725.

The first bridge to cross Little Bay (from Newington to Durham) was the Piscataqua Bridge, constructed as a private concern by patriotic investors in 1794. The bridge stretched from Fox Point to Goat Island and across Little Bay to Durham. In the early 1800s the traveler crossing the bay by carriage could continue on to the new capitol of Concord by means of a turnpike built to connect the Piscataqua with the interior part of the state.

The traveler by ferry—or today, by auto—crossing from Bloody Point to Dover Point must decide between many routes for exploration. Should one proceed north to Dover following the Cocheco River (and Route 16), then beyond to Rochester? Again going north, the traveler could also decide to skip the Cocheco for the Salmon Falls River, hoping to spy one of the river's namesakes as the water descends from Somersworth on the Maine border. An alternative journey on Route 4 west to Durham follows the beautiful Oyster River. To make the decision more demanding, the Great Bay lies to the south of Dover Point. Numerous rivers and streams feed this fresh and salt water estuary. The Lamprey River takes one deep into the heart of New Hampshire, passing first by the old mill town of Newmarket. Further south, the Squamscott River flows into Great Bay. Up the Squamscott you find Exeter, one of the most picturesque of New England towns.

"Salamagundi Shop", 17 Locust Street, Dover

The sea deeply affects the environs of the towns surrounding the Great Bay. Tidal lands abound. In the drive along Route 101 to Exeter, the marshes of the Squamscott Valley seem reminiscent of Hampton on the coast, yet Exeter is a dozen miles inland. Exeter was an early shipbuilding and mill center, the town forming in the 1600s around the falls of the Squamscott River. During the American Revolution, Exeter was temporarily the revolutionary capitol of New Hampshire, supplanting the provincial capitol of Portsmouth. At Exeter, the New Hampshire General Court met, wrote, and rewrote several versions of the new state constitution until they finally got it right. Exeter produced one famous son of the Revolution, Enoch Poor, a merchant and shipbuilder who became a brigadier-general during the war, though he failed to survive it. In 1781 philanthropist John Phillips founded

Exeter, date unknown

Phillips-Exeter Academy, which has grown over the centuries into a multifaceted campus that dominates the town, bringing college-bound youth and their families to Exeter in order to prepare the students for the academic rigors and social demands of the Ivy League. The people of Exeter maintain an air of pride and privilege, evident when visiting some of the established institutions of the town. For example, dominating the center of Exeter is the First Congregational Church, an imposing white clapboard structure with the requisite black shutters and elegant steeple. The present building dates back to 1781. The interior is just as historical and very formal. Christ is well-dressed and extravagantly polite at this parish.

Painting of Daniel Webster by Joseph Ames, 1852

Daniel Webster (1782–1852)

New Hampshire's most illustrious native son was born in Franklin, New Hampshire, educated at Phillips-Exeter Academy in Exeter and Dartmouth College in Hanover, and lived in Portsmouth from 1807 to 1816. Daniel Webster was a trial lawyer and firm Federalist who resisted the Democrat-Republican domination of the presidency and congress during the first quarter of the nineteenth century. Webster became a leader of the Whig Party, a congressman from New Hampshire, and a senator from Massachusetts. He also served as Secretary of State. Charles Brewster penned the following portrait of Daniel Webster. It appeared in one of Brewster's newspaper columns, subsequently titled *Rambles About Portsmouth*:

Daniel Webster, in 1807, became a resident of Portsmouth, and looking upon this as his future location, he arranged for those domestic relations which make a residence a home; and in June 1808, was married to the tenderly beloved Grace Fletcher, who remained his partner for nineteen years. They occupied first the house now owned by Robert Gray in Vaughan street. In the fire of 1813, they were residents of a house on Pleasant street, in front of Richard Jenness's mansion. This house afterwards occupied the house next north of the residence of Charles H. Ladd, on High street. Mr. Webster's office was on the west side of Market street, over the store now occupied by Mr. Stavers.

Mr. Webster came not among us as a young lawyer.—Though but twenty-five years of age, his noble form, his manly boldness and his maturity of mind, readily commanded the attention and respect of more advanced years. His influence was not only felt in the court-room, but as a citizen he was ever looked to for counsel; and to the calls of philanthropy no ear was ever more open or hand more free. Here were developed those peculiar qualifications which afterwards exhibited him as the statesman who would do honor to any nation. It was while residing here that his own State placed him in the council of the nation; and at a time, too, when the elements of politics were burning more fiercely than they have since. The confidence reposed in him was found not to be misplaced, and after serving one term he was re-elected. In 1816, after a residence in Portsmouth of nine years, he moved to Boston.

Newmarket Mill, at the Newmarket Manufacturing Company, Main Street

Newmarket is another town of the Great Bay built at the falls of the Lamprey River. Newmarket was, like Exeter, a shipbuilding and mill center. After 1800 the town fully embraced the Industrial Revolution, developing large, imposing red-brick factories where thousands labored to produce the domestic goods of a growing American populace. At one point during the heyday of the Industrial Revolution, Newmarket boasted the largest factory building in the world. Today the town's old factories have been converted to offices and condominiums.

Adjacent to Newmarket is Durham, once called Oyster River after the river that rises and falls with the tide. Durham was noteworthy in the colonial period for being the site of numerous massacres perpetrated by French-instigated Native Americans against the British-American inhabitants. The most famous general New Hampshire (with the exception of John Stark) of the Revolutionary War, John Sullivan, lived in a large clapboard house next to the Oyster River. Sullivan gained a reputation for his role in the attack on Fort William and Mary in 1774. He served in Rhode Island and won important victories against the Iroquois of upstate New York. He also served as president of New Hampshire. Since the mid-nineteenth century, Durham has been noteworthy as the home of the University of New Hampshire. For over a century the hilly, forested environs of Durham have accommodated a growing number of university buildings. Walking about this campus among the woods is a delightful experience.

The surrounding towns of Lee and Madbury still resemble the eighteenth-century rural colonial past. Not so the city of Dover, founded in the early 1600s on the Cocheco River. The falls of the Cocheco allowed Dover to become an important lumber and shipbuilding center, then after 1800 a factory center. Dover was the home, for twenty years, of the great historian of New Hampshire, Jeremy Belknap.

Jeremy and Ruth Belknap

The Reverend Jeremy Belknap was one of the intellectual leaders of Northern New England during the Revolutionary period. A native of Boston, the Harvard College graduate migrated north to New Hampshire in 1764, serving as a schoolteacher in Portsmouth and Greenland. In 1767 he accepted the call of Dover's First Parish to become their pastor and served the parish for twenty years. Belknap was a warm patriot during the American Revolution who nevertheless believed that Christian values should temper America's military, political, and economic objectives. A political and moral conservative, Belknap repeatedly opposed excess during the war. He believed that God ordained American victory; the victors must not destroy and alienate the vanquished. Belknap was vocal in his support of the American loyalists. Some eyebrows were raised due to his friendship with the last royal governor of New Hampshire, John Wentworth. Yet Belknap's goal was peace and harmony rather than political advantage. Believing that the human and natural past, rather than grand ideologies and political interest, should always guide human affairs, Belknap penned a three

Jeremy Belknap's Assessment of the New Hampshire Shakers, 1784

Jeremy Belknap was a traditional Congregational minister who was intolerant toward other religious beliefs that, in his opinion, were based on nonsense. The Shakers, a New England religious sect given to extravagant claims, incorporated eschatology into astronomy, and claimed (according to Belknap) that the aurora borealis, a frequent phenomenon seen in the New Hampshire night sky, "are entirely ceased." Belknap wondered in a letter to his friend Ebenezer Hazard: "Have you any of those creatures in Pennsylvania?" When on one occasion in the spring of 1784 Belknap witnessed the astonishing light show of the aurora borealis, he tossed off a letter to Hazard with the evidence to prove that the Shakers were

> *false prophets.* They have come within six miles of us, and perform their agitations with a volatility and flexibility which the ignorant observers can account for only by witchcraft. It is confidently said, and I believe it is true, that one of their late meetings was introduced by handing round a bottle of rum; of which each taking a large draught became *inspired.*

On another occasion Belknap wrote to his friend: "There are a few of them at Barrington, about 6 or 7 miles from here, and another parcel at a place called Loudon, which is near the confluence of the Pemigewasset and Winnipiseoge Rivers, and some at Massabesick, in the county of York," in Maine. "They have strange postures and actions; the common opinion is that they are under the power of *witchcraft.* This is the usual way (among ignorant people) of solving every uncommon appearance." One Shaker belief fascinated Belknap. They believe "that they are judges of the world, and that the dead are daily rising, and coming before them to be judged." Many sinners had appeared before them, such as George Fox and George Whitefield, both of whom were "absolved from their errors, and are now at rest."

—Belknap Papers
Massachusetts Historical Society

volume *History of New-Hampshire* in which he tried to assess objectively New Hampshire's human history and provide an enduring portrait of its natural history. Like most early American ministers, Belknap was a polymath interested in studying most human and natural phenomena. He was a geographer of note and an explorer as well, organizing the first scientific expedition to the White Mountains in 1784.

Engraving of Jeremy Belknap

Little known but just as interesting was the life of Belknap's wife, the former Ruth Eliot of Boston. The Eliots were an old New England family who were religious leaders in colonial Massachusetts. Ruth's uncle Andrew Eliot and cousin John Eliot were important religious and intellectual leaders of Boston before, during, and after the American Revolution. Ruth was genteel, well-read, and urbane. Growing up in Boston she could have scarcely imagined living anywhere else, much less the New Hampshire frontier. The past hides from us how Jeremy and Ruth met. But by the time Jeremy earned his Bachelors degree at Harvard in 1762, he and Ruth were already "dearest friends." When Jeremy unexpectedly went to Portsmouth to teach school and study with the Reverend Samuel Haven, pastor of the South Parish, and began to fill in at the pulpit of neighboring Piscataqua parishes, Ruth waited patiently in Boston. When Jeremy received the call to become pastor at Dover's First Parish, he

The Parson's Wife

Ruth Belknap, wife of the Dover minister Jeremy Belknap, was born and raised in Boston in a respectable, genteel family. It was quite a shock when she followed her fiancé to Dover to become his wife. Dover was a rural community on the New Hampshire frontier. Frustrated but unwilling to let her situation in life destroy a sense of humor, she penned the following poem:

> Dear Cousin,—It is now Thanksgiving Night, and I should be thankful indeed if I could call and spend the evening with you, or have some agreeable friend call in upon me, but as this cannot be, I must converse this way. I have had frequent opportunities to Boston this fall, but expect this will be the last for some time: therefore am willing to improve it. And I think for your amusement I will send you 'The Pleasures of a Country Life,' written when I had a true taste of them by having no maid.

> Up in the morning I must rise
> Before I've time to rub my eyes,
> With half-pin'd gown, unbuckled shoe,
> I haste to milk my lowing cow.
> But, Oh! It makes my heart to ake,
> I have no bread till I can bake,
> And then, alas! It makes me sputter,
> For I must churn or have no butter.
> The hogs with swill too I must serve;
> For hogs must eat or men will starve.
> Besides, my spouse can get no cloaths
> Unless I much offend my nose.
> For all that try it know it's true
> There is no smell like colouring blue.
> Then round the parish I must ride
> And make enquiry far and wide
> To find some girl that is a spinner,
> Then hurry home to get my dinner.
> If with romantic steps I stray
> Around the fields and meadows gay,
> The grass, besprinkled with the dews,
> Will wet my feet and rot my shoes.
> If on a mossy bank I sleep
> Pismires and crickets o'er me creep,
> Or near the purling rill am seen
> There dire musquitos pierce my skin.
> Yet such delights I seldom see
> Confin'd to house and family.

All summer long I toil & sweat,
Blister my hands, and scold & fret.
And when the summer's work is o'er,
New toils arise from Autumn's store.
Corn must be husk'd and pork be kill'd,
The house with all confusion fill'd.
O could you see the grand display
Upon our annual butchering day,—
See me look like ten thousand sluts,
My kitchen spread with grease & guts,—
You'd lift your hands surpris'd, & swear
That Mother Trisket's self were there.
Yet starch'd up folks that live in town,
That lounge upon your beds till noon,
That never tire yourselves with work,
Unless with handling knife & fork,
Come, see the sweets of country life,
Display'd in Parson B————'s wife.

By way of postscript, Jeremy Belknap wrote his friend Ebenezer Hazard about the verse: "I assure you she says the one half was not told. She might now write *the second part of the same tune*, and entitle it the *Progress of Misery*. It is better, however, to laugh at our misfortunes than to sink under the pressure of them."

—Belknap Papers
Massachusetts Historical Society

asked for her hand, received it, and the two set up housekeeping in Dover.

Dover was, for Ruth Eliot Belknap, quite a shock. Whereas Boston was a busy port city of 25,000 people, Dover was a sleepy mill town of 1,500. The society in Boston included wealthy merchants such as the Hancocks, brilliant theologians such as Charles Chauncy, and women of polish and elegance. Jeremy and Ruth Belknap were the social, intellectual, and cultural leaders of Dover. Ruth grew to be very lonely. There were children, however; Ruth bore six in nine years. Father and mother were blessed that all of them survived infancy. Jeremy was frequently kind enough to let Ruth return to Boston for visits of several weeks where the sea air and sights and sounds of the port city invigorated and renewed her.

Ruth Eliot Belknap was a delicate soul, given to fatigue and nervousness. The passing years of motherhood and her relative seclusion in Dover's "wooden" world weighed upon her. When war came to New England in April 1775 at Lexington and Concord Massachusetts, Jeremy rushed to Boston to assist his parents and sister. He was successful in bringing them from the beleaguered city to Dover, where they added to a steadily growing brood of children. John, the fifth child, was born in 1776, and Andrew, their sixth, in 1779. The Belknap's two-story, white clapboard home could scarcely accommodate eleven people. And the privation of war made it doubly hard to feed them. Like most congregational ministers, Belknap had a fixed salary according to a contractual agreement with his parish. This yearly salary did not change, even when the price of goods and depreciating currency during wartime did. Inflation made Belknap's salary of £125 seem practically worthless. The people of Dover were hit hard as well—they simply could not afford to adjust the pastor's salary. By war's end they were unable to meet their obligation toward Rev. Belknap.

Ruth and Jeremy did everything they could to survive the war and its aftermath. The town of Dover suspended public school during the war, so the Belknaps looked elsewhere to educate their children, particularly their sons. As a poor pastor with neither title nor fortune, and without the funds to send their firstborn Josey (as he was affectionately called) to Harvard, Belknap's alma mater, the father had little choice but to apprentice the son to a craftsman in Philadelphia.

But Belknap had heard reports that Philadelphia "generally, if not always," had the smallpox. In the eighteenth century, cautious people who had faith in science and medicine inoculated themselves and their children. The process of inoculation was a primitive form of vaccination: It led to the illness in a less virulent, usually non-fatal form, that insured future immunity—yet it required several weeks of quarantine. There were no facilities for such a process in New Hampshire nor, surprisingly, in Boston. During the war Portsmouth had reserved a small island in the Piscataqua to quarantine those people with smallpox or those undergoing the long trial of inoculation. But with war's end Pest Island, as it was called, was abandoned and physicians ceased inoculating patients.

For the Belknaps, the *solution* was to have their son inoculated in Philadelphia, the scientific capitol of early America. Most Americans before 1800 rarely had the luxury of such preventative medicine. Indeed *physick*, as the practice of medicine was called, remained primitive until the mid-nineteenth century. Until then most medicine in New Hampshire was based on home remedies of varying quality and efficacy, a *materia medica* derived largely from hearsay and tradition, and attention from physicians without medical training or any other credentials save their adoption of the title and purchase of the tools of the profession. Few cities had hospitals before 1800; New Hampshire's first hospital, built in Concord in 1842, was initially termed an insane asylum. One of the top medical facilities in the nation today, the Dartmouth-Hitchcock Hospital and Medical School in Hanover, New Hampshire, did not have its start until the late 1800s.

Jeremy Belknap, like most eighteenth-century congregational ministers, wore many hats, one of which was that of scientist. Typically the most educated person in small towns, the minister was the expert on all intellectual matters: politics, history, the weather, and medicine. Belknap kept diaries and memoranda in which he recorded numerous remedies for every conceivable illness, from worms to malaria to "throat distempers." He was a medical statistician of sorts, recording the marriages, births (whether live or dead), baptisms, and deaths of all the people of Dover. He was intrigued by cases of longevity and wondered what in a person's habits led to long life. He kept records of the weather, forming, as it were, volumes of personal almanacs of daily meteorological conditions. He kept up with politics and frequently used the pulpit as would a journalist a newspaper and a politician a rostrum. The pulpit was also the best way to teach parishioners about the past. Belknap conceived it to be a natural avocation of the minister to engage in historical research and writing. To this end he spent twenty years researching and writing *The History of New-Hampshire*, the story of the human quest to wrestle a settled existence from the harsh natural environment of a land of plentiful rivers, deep snows, vast wilderness forests, and numerous craggy peaks.

New Hampshire's Dark Day

Jeremy Belknap wrote his good friend Ebenezer Hazard in early June 1780 to describe the remarkable phenomenon of nature witnessed a fortnight earlier, "I mean *the darkness* which overspread almost the whole of New England on the 19th of May. As I am no theorist, I shall not trouble you with any conjectures, but shall rather give you a detail of such *facts* as either fell under my own observation or are creditably evidenced by others." The darkness caused amazement, consternation, and fascination throughout the states of New England. Some people thought it a supernatural event; Belknap examined it in typical American scientific fashion. He relied chiefly on his own observations, supplemented with the observations and anecdotes of others, the validity of which he sifted through his own common sense.

It was a typical sunny spring day until noon, when darkness spread sufficiently that by early afternoon candles were lit and kept burning the remainder of the day. "It was not the darkness of a thunder-cloud, but a vapour like the smoke of a malt-house or a coal-kiln, and there was a strong smell of smoke the whole day, as there had been for some days before." There had been little recent rain, and it was the time of year "for burning the woods to plant corn on the new lands." In recent days the air was smoky; it was often difficult to see, and sunlight disappeared a "half an hour before setting." Several days before the event "I well remember that.... every part of our house was full of smoke, as well as all the surrounding air, and I examined to see if it proceeded from our own fire, but was satisfied it was the same vapour that the air was full of."

Notwithstanding the fantastic accounts of others, Belknap studied the matter enough to know the cause of the darkness was simply smoke. He provided Hazard with a brief detailing of the evidence upon which his conclusion was based. For example "Colonel Hazzen, of the Continental troops, was riding in the woods somewhere about Pennicook, and in the *low grounds* the vapour was so thick that it was difficult to fetch his breath." Also, "small birds, such as sparrows and yellow-birds, were found dead in divers places; and some flew into the houses, very probably to avoid the suffocating vapour." As for the extent,

Belknap wrote acquaintances to discover just how far the smoke spread.

"Shall I now entertain you with the whims and apprehensions of mankind upon this unusual appearance? It is not surprizing that the vulgar should turn it all into prodigy and miracle; but what would you think of men of sense, and of a liberal education," who said, as did one local clergyman, "that it was the fulfilling of Joel's prophecy of a 'pillar of smoke'" found in the Old Testament? "Another wondered at me for not placing this phenomenon in the same rank with [the ancient historian] Josephus's signs of the destruction of Jerusalem" in 70 A. D. One drew from it inspiration to explain the mysteries of the Book of Revelation. "Another... called his congregation together during the darkness, and prayed that the sun might shine again." Those with fewer religious proclivities thought to explain it as the "earth... passing through the tail of a comet.... How many more extravagant conceptions have been formed by men, whose minds one would think had been enlarged by reason and philosophy, I know not. Doubtless you will hear enough on your return to make you stand amazed at the power which fear and superstition have over the minds of men."

—Jeremy Belknap to Ebenezer Hazard,
June 5, 1780
Massachusetts Historical Society

3

FOLLOWING THE PATHS OF RANGERS

A large part of the first volume of Jeremy Belknap's *History of New-Hampshire* details the numerous military conflicts between the French and their Native American allies and the British-American colonists that plagued the region of the Great Bay and Piscataqua Valley from 1689 to 1763. On one occasion in 1694, 94 people of the Oyster River settlement (Durham) lost their lives. The New Hampshire colonists retaliated by sending small bands of rangers, made up of town militiamen, into the northern forest to destroy (and scalp) the enemy Algonquins. Some of the bloodiest exploits in colonial American military history occurred because of the action of these ranger companies.

Most famous were the deeds of Major Robert Rogers and his band of New Hampshire rangers who fought during the French-Indian War. In the autumn of 1759 Rogers, in response to the ongoing Native American attacks on New Hampshire towns, led his rangers north from Lake Champlain to the St. Francis River in Canada, where they attacked the St. Francis Indians on one October morning. The village was taken by surprise, though the casualties among the Native Americans were women and children and the aged more than the warriors. Having plundered and burnt the village, Rogers and the rangers retreated, fleeing French and Native American forces south to Lake Memphremagog in northern Vermont then on to the Connecticut River, which some of the rangers— those who escaped the French and Native Americans and the privation of the stingy forest—used to return to the fort at Number Four.

Less famous yet as bloody was the Battle of Lovewell's Pond, which occurred during Dummer's War. In the spring of 1725, Captain John Lovewell led a company of rangers north into the foothills of the White Mountains.

Robert Rogers (1731–1795)

Robert Rogers, although he was born in Massachusetts and died in England, will forever be associated with New Hampshire because of his daring military exploits during the French-Indian War and because of his infamy earned thereafter. Rogers grew up in Rumford, New Hampshire, the scene of Native American attacks in the 1740s during King George's War. At the beginning of the French-Indian War in 1755, Rogers showed himself to be an engaging leader and fearless soldier. He was made captain of rangers to scout enemy positions and to make quick attacks and rapid retreats. Rogers is most famous for leading his rangers in October 1759 to attack the St. Francis Indians of Canada. Rogers destroyed the village, but not all of the warriors, who along with French soldiers pursued the rangers as they retreated south to Vermont and New Hampshire. Some companies of retreating rangers, including Rogers himself, used the Connecticut River to take them back to the shelter of the Fort at Number 4.

Rogers' subsequent career featured some success and many failures. Rogers was sent to the Great Lakes to accept the surrender of Detroit from the French and later was commissioned commander of the British fort at Michilimackinac in the beautiful if lonely narrows between Lake Michigan and Lake Huron. Rogers' wife, Elizabeth Browne, daughter of the Reverend Arthur Browne, priest at Queen's Chapel in Portsmouth, accompanied him to Michilimackinac. In the end, however, Rogers was a difficult man to live with. His mounting debts and rejection of the American cause during the War for Independence forced her to obtain a divorce from the New Hampshire General Court. Rogers spent time in debtor's prison and died a pauper in 1795.

Overall Rogers was an eccentric genius of unbridled energy and unsatisfied restlessness. His *A Concise Account of North America* provides a unique description of New England. Included is Rogers' account of the White Mountains, the largest of which, Mount Washington, he tried to ascend but had to turn back defeated because of the unexpected height and dense fog. Likewise, Rogers never quite achieved the summit of his own potential.

Memorable accounts of Rogers' life were rendered by the novelist Kenneth Roberts in *Northwest Passage* and by Spencer Tracy in a 1940 film of the same name.

They stopped to build a makeshift fort at Ossipee Lake before proceeding to the Pequawket encampment situated in the Saco River valley between Conway and Fryeburg, just over the Maine border. A visitor can generally follow their route driving north on Route 16 to Route 302. Route 16 cuts a path from Dover north to Rochester, paralleling the descending Cocheco River, then further north on a line between Lake Winnipesaukee and Maine. The road travels through Wakefield, Ossipee, Tamworth, and Chocorua, then northeast to Conway and the Saco River. At Fryeburg the Pequawkets, led by Paugus, ambushed Lovewell and his men, killing the captain and many others besides. The Battle of Lovewell's Pond was immediately commemorated by histories, epics, songs, and a growing fanciful tradition that turned Lovewell and his fallen comrades into great heroes of the New Hampshire and Maine frontier.

At the same time other ranger companies marched north into the White Mountains, forging trails that would later become well-marked roads and eventually highways that followed descending rivers such as the Saco, Ellis, Peabody, Androscoggin, Ammonoosuc, and Pemigewasset. In 1725 Captain Samuel Willard led a ranger company through the mountains along what would today be the Kancamagus Highway, an exciting drive that connects North Woodstock and Conway, generally paralleling the clear and cold mountain spring, Swift River, as it descends to the Saco River. Mount Kancamagus, named for the Penacook chief and grandnephew of Passaconaway, looms just to the south. Other nearby mountains commemorate famous Native American leaders. Mount Chocorua, a 3475 foot peak with a distinct rocky pinnacle, serves as a beacon for travelers going north on Route 16. Chocorua, according to legend, died at the hands of an avenging colonist on the summit that bears his name. Mount Paugus, due west, recalls the life of the Pequawket warrior. West of Paugus stands the 4,060 foot Mount Passaconaway, named for the Penacook chief who was said to haunt the White Mountains, particularly Mount Washington.

Another ranger company intent on surprising and scalping the descendants of Passaconaway approached the White Mountains from the Ammonoosuc River valley. Led by Captain Thomas Wells, these rangers sought

Benjamin Champney's 1863 painting "A Quiet Storm" depicts
New Hampshire's Saco River

The Legend of Chocorua

The traveler journeying north on Route 16 toward the White Mountains gets his first idea of what is to come when glimpsing the picturesque horned peak Mount Chocorua, named to commemorate the tragic death of the mountain's namesake:

> Chocorua, another of the chiefs who remained after his tribe had left the country, has given his name to one of the peaks on the extreme boundary of the White Mountains. It is a singularly-shaped mountain, its top rising up like a tower crowned by turrets at its corners. To the south the ascent of the summit is perpendicular, rising up smooth rock some hundred feet.
>
> To this, tradition says, Chocorua had retreated, pursued by a miserable white hunter. To the highest point he had climbed, and there he stood unarmed, while below, and within gunshot, stood his pursuer. Chocorua besought the hunter not to kill him. He plead his friendliness to the whites, and the harmless, scattered condition of his few followers. But the hardened hunter was unmoved; the price of his scalp was too tempting; gold plead stronger than the poor Native American. Seeing that he should avail nothing, the noble chieftain, raising himself up, stretched forth his arms, and called upon the Gods of his fathers to curse the land. Then, casting a defiant glance at his pursuer, he leaped from the brink of the precipice on the south side to the rocks below. And to this day, say the inhabitants, a malignant disease has carried off the cattle that they have attempted rearing around this mountain.
>
> —Benjamin G. Willey
> *Incidents in White Mountain History (1856)*

retaliation for the many Native American attacks on Deerfield, Massachusetts, Wells' hometown. The Ammonoosuc is a short-lived river in length but not in spirit and beauty. It rises in the tallest peaks of the White Mountains—the Presidentials, the highest being Mount Washington, surrounded by Mount Adams and Mount Jefferson. In Thomas Wells' time these peaks were an utter wilderness known collectively by the Native American name of Agiocochook.

Today's Route 302 parallels the Ammonoosuc on its western descent from the White Mountains until it flows into the Connecticut River. Along this path Captain Wells led rangers in April 1725. The Ammonoosuc took the men into a region dominated by massive walls of granite and narrow defiles. Wells and his men entered into one of the defiles, a beautiful notch between peaks. The traveler today knows it as Crawford Notch; in Wells' time it was known as the Western Notch. The rangers blazed a trail through the Notch known until then only to Native Americans and found themselves surrounded by massive mountains on all sides. The motorist driving Route 302 south knows the exact same feeling. Mount Washington looms to the east, its distant summit seeming to be a lifetime away. One can hike established trails maintained by the Appalachian Mountain Club, or take the tram, built in 1859, that chugs its way to the top. But Wells and his men had none of these luxuries.

On April 18, 1725, they made the ascent. Deep snow lay packed on some parts of the slope. In an account that Captain Wells wrote of the journey, he noted that although in the valley it was a warm April day on the summit of the mountain it was clear, windy, and icy cold. The pond on the summit was frozen. The cold was so unbearable that they could not stay but had to descend from the summit quickly. Before departure they reveled in the extensive view of New Hampshire. Wells and his men could see most of the state's important landmarks. Mount Washington is infamous for having bad, even dangerous weather. The highest wind speed of 231 miles per hour was recorded at Mount Washington in 1932. Even in summer the volatile atmosphere can turn ugly and send down icy rain and snow. To have a clear day where the summit is not shrouded in clouds or haze was remarkably good luck for Captain Wells. They were able to see Lake Winnipesaukee to the south; the Green Mountains to the west (in Vermont); the rivers descending from the White Mountains such as the Ammonoosuc flowing west; the Saco beginning its long journey to Maine from the western slopes of Mount Washington; the Peabody, a tributary of one of Maine's important rivers, the Androscoggin, which the men could also clearly see; and the Ellis, flowing from the Eastern (Pinkham) Notch south to merge with the Saco River at Conway. Even the distant Atlantic Ocean was visible.

In fact it was because sailors off the coasts of Maine,

New Hampshire, and Massachusetts could see the distant white peaks that the first settlers were seized with a desire to penetrate and ascend the highest of these mountains. To some explorers such as John Smith, the mountains twinkled. To Captain Christopher Levett sailing along the coast in 1623, the mountains looked like crystal. The early colonists believed that the White Mountains must hold something valuable to make them glimmer so. Native American legends of carbuncles (gems) on the summit seemed to confirm the idea of wealth to be had by the adventurer willing to brace the wilderness challenge. Darby Field, who lived in the Oyster River area around Great Bay, developed such a yearning. In 1642 Field ascended the Saco River to Pequawket lands at what is today the upper Saco region of Fryeburg, Maine, and Conway, New Hampshire. Field then turned north, following the Ellis River to the plateau on the east side of Mount Washington. Today's explorer can parallel Field's feat by driving Route 16 to Pinkham Notch, where one can find the Appalachian Mountain Club firmly entrenched with maps, guides, accommodations, and food—all of which Field lacked. Accompanied by two Pequawket braves, Field ascended Mount Washington from the east, probably going up by way of Boott Spur. It was summer and a clear day, so he could make out rivers, lakes, and the blue Atlantic. Field lugged back crystal stones that turned out to be worthless.

But Field returned again later that summer. Thomas Gorges and Richard Vines, two adventurers from Maine, ascended the mountain as well during the fall of 1642. Gorges and Vines worked for the Maine proprietor Ferdinando Gorges.

After the several ascents of the mountain in 1642, no one on record visited the White Mountains for twenty years, when John Josselyn, an English physician and botanist, visited his brother Henry Josselyn on the Maine coast. Henry was another agent in the service of Gorges and Mason. While in Maine he had frequent dealings with his New Hampshire neighbors to the south. His brother John used his visits in the 1630s and again in the 1660s as an opportunity to explore northern New England. On one occasion, sometime during his second visit, John journeyed to and ascended the Great Mountain (Mount Washington), becoming the first scientist to do so. Josselyn and unnamed companions climbed the eastern slope, found snow along the way, and came to the pond at the summit, from which they "beheld a vapor like a great pillar drawn up by the sun-beams out of a great lake or pond into the air where it was formed into a cloud. The country beyond these hills northward is daunting terrible being full of rocky hills as thick as mole hills in a meadow and clothed with infinite thick woods."

THE BELKNAP-CUTLER EXPEDITION

Scientists did not ascend Mount Washington again until 1784, when Jeremy Belknap, Manasseh Cutler, Daniel Little, Joshua Fisher, and Joseph Whipple followed the Ellis upriver to Pinkham Notch. These scientists were patriots who believed that, with the War for American Independence having just concluded in 1783, there was a need for Americans to journey inland and up mountains to discover the natural productions of America and to establish a scientific footing for subsequent geologists, botanists, geographers, and natural historians.

The journey took place at the end of July, 1784. The men set out from Conway, a settlement then about twenty years old situated at the confluence of the Saco and Swift rivers. Route 16, which parallels the Ellis River from Conway to Pinkham Notch, was in 1784 a wilderness trail. The guide of the Belknap-Cutler Expedition was a backwoodsman named Captain John Evans, who was one of the first settlers of the region, a noted hunter, trailblazer, and road-builder. What is today Route 16 was originally called the Shelburne Road after John Evans and a team of ax-men blazed the trail in 1774. At that time, Evans and others ascended the Great Mountain. Ten years later Evans was back, following the Shelburne Road, which was but an infrequently used trail in the woods. Belknap, who kept a detailed journal of the expedition, described the Shelburne Road as

> one that was cut ten years ago, and has been disused
> for several years; and 'tis now grown up with bushes
> as high as a man's head on horseback, full of wind-
> fallen trees, deep mires, and broken bridges; and in

one place a tornado had so torn up the trees that we
laboured with excessive difficulty to get through with
our horses.

Captain Evans led the men along the course of the Ellis
River on the east side of the mountains to a grassy meadow
high above sea level that sat in the shadow of the Great
Mountain, at the origin of several important New England
rivers. The ax-man Evans constructed a sturdy hut of
evergreen poles and branches, under which they slept in
expectation of the next day's journey.

According to Belknap, the men began their ascent on
Saturday, July 24, just after six in the morning. The
scientists (or rather, the guides) carried with them
barometers, thermometers, a telescope, and a sextant, with
which to perform a variety of laudable scientific
experiments. In particular, they wanted to calculate the
latitude and elevation of the Great Mountain to show
without a doubt that America, too, produces grand and
wonderful phenomena. But by the time they reached the
summit, many of the instruments were broken. And not
everyone reached the summit. Joshua Fisher experienced a
terrible pain in his side soon after they began the ascent.
Shortly after Fisher turned back, Belknap, who had been
huffing and puffing all the way, finally found his "breath,
legs, and overall strength give out," not even half way up.
He realized that if he continued, by the top he "should be
fit for nothing but to lie down and sleep." Belknap
"consented to come down alone," comforting himself "with
that old adage, To be willing is noble enough." Making the
best of his lonely and depressing circumstances, Belknap
did a bit of exploring on his own, and found a beautiful and
awesome wall of black, "square-faced stones, laid as fair
and regular as a piece of masonry, the water trickling out
from between them."

He reached the base camp by mid-morning. After a
meal and a nap, he and Fisher, partners in failure,
wandered about the meadow, discovering an abandoned
beaver dam. "It was old and firm, and overgrown with
alders; we could see no trace of their cabbin." To their own
"cabin" the men repaired at dusk; they put additional
hemlock branches on the roof to protect it from the rain,
which was falling. Despite their precautions, the hut leaked

and the fire threatened to go out. They spent a long, wet, dismal night, constantly wondering where their friends were.

The others, meanwhile, continued the ascent. Evans led the scientists up Cutler's River through several zones of vegetation. As they ascended, the evergreens came to dominate the deciduous trees; soon, however, the evergreens gave out, replaced by short disfigured bushes called krummholz. Eventually nearing the summit, they found an alpine environment of moss-covered rocks hosting flora usually found much further north in Canada. They reached the summit by early afternoon. There they found themselves in an inhospitable situation. The wind was piercing and cold. Clouds surrounded them, obscured the view, prevented scientific measurements, then brought an icy fog that so enveloped the men that they realized their desperate condition and the necessity to descend quickly. The guides, unfortunately, had lost their way, and were

Northern peaks and Great Gulf from the Mount Washington summit

unsure how to proceed. Their compasses behaved erratically. Their hands numb, their bodies exhausted, their minds uneasy, they guessed the trail. Their guess proved to be the correct direction, but one so precarious that their chief guide, Captain Evans, took a wrong step and slid three hundred feet, fortunately without serious injury. The others, forced to seek an alternative route, did so successfully, rejoining the captain at the tree line about dusk. They built a hasty "fire, and by the side of it stood or lay during the night, parboiled and smoke-dried." The next day they found their way back to camp.

After a brief rest, they proceeded north then west of the mountains on overgrown paths toward Joseph Whipple's plantation at Dartmouth (now Jefferson), New Hampshire. According to Jeremy Belknap, the road, which today is made concrete by Route 16 North and Route 2 West, was

> worse than what we had travelled on Friday. The
> greatest expedition we could make was two miles in
> an hour, and in some parts not so much. We kept one
> man before [Captain Evans] with an ax, to cut away
> windfalls, or limbs of windfalls, over many of which
> we leaped our horses, and under many crawled, and
> went round the tops or roots of many more, and over
> many broken or rotten bridges, and through many
> deep sloughs; and, to aid the difficulty, we met with
> an heavy shower, of two hours' continuance, which
> wet us every one to the skin, and after all were
> obliged, by the approach to night, to stop eight miles
> short of our object, and encamp on the wet ground
> under a bark tent hastily constructed by the side of a
> large fire made to windward of our tabernacle, so
> that, if we raised our heads a foot from the ground,
> we were suffocated.

Belknap kept up his spirits the best he could with healthy
doses of chocolate. The next day, Monday, they arrived at
Whipple's home, which often masqueraded as a stockade
and a tavern, depending upon the intentions of travelers
who knocked at his door. The men arrived wet and tired.
Whipple's place was situated

> in the midst of a vast amphitheatre, surrounded on all
> sides but the N.W. by cloudcap't mountains. The
> view was grand. The vapours were rising in
> innumerable columns from the sides of the
> mountains, and converging toward their summits,
> forming into clouds, and then descending in showers,
> after a while reascending as before, and thus keeping
> up a constant circulation.

For a brief moment, the mountains were partially free of
cloud-cover; Belknap sketched them so to recover the
image more efficiently later back home.

"Tuesday, July 27. Cloudy morning." Storms threatened,
then arrived during a hasty church service in a barn where
thirty-eight people heard Belknap preach on the first book
of Corinthians. It was the first sermon ever given at
Dartmouth. Eight children were baptized. Other more
corporeal pleasures consisted of the joys of maple sugar,

The Legend of Nancy Barton

The story of the tragic death of Nancy Barton, the young maid-servant working for Colonel Joseph Whipple, has become one of the most oft-told stories of the New Hampshire past:

Nancy Barton is supposed to have been the first white woman who passed through the Notch of the White Hills voluntarily. She was employed to keep a boarding-house for lumbermen in Jefferson; was industrious, faithful, and toiled early and late for small wages. Her employer was taken captive by the Native Americans and she served them liquor until they were all helpless; then cut the thongs with which he was bound and secured his liberty. She carefully husbanded her earnings, and in time had laid down a handsome sum. She was engaged to be married to one of the workmen and arrangements were made for them to proceed to Portsmouth, her native place, where they were to be united and make a home. She trustingly, but unwisely, placed her money in the hands of her affianced, and began making preparations for her journey. This having become known to her employer, he determined not to lose so valuable a housekeeper, and to circumvent the marriage he sent her away on errands to Lancaster. This was meanness beyond description, and the result was tragic. During her absence her professed lover left the locality with a party going south, taking her money away with him. She somehow heard of this affair on the same day, and quickly matured plans for pursuit. With a bundle of clothing she hastened down the snow-covered trail, guided by the trees spotted for that purpose, and after a weary journey of thirty miles, having traveled all night through a dark forest, she reached the spot where the party had camped. The fire had gone out.; Benumbed with cold, she knelt about the charred brands and tried in vain to blow from them a flame. Again she took up her weary march, fording the icy waters of the Saco several times, until exhausted nature succumbed to cold and fatigue and she sank down to rise no more. [...] A relief party had been hurried forward after the storm of snow came on, but they were too far behind to save her life; her rigid body was found buried under the drifting snow upon the south side of the stream in Bartlett, since known as "Nancy's brook." Her faithless lover learned of her sad fate, and being seized with keen remorse for his crime, became hopelessly insane and ended his days by a miserable death. [...] Grim Justice could find no doom too dark as a penalty for such crime. The early inhabitants believed the ghost of Nancy Barton's betrayer and robber lingered about the brookside where she perished, and that his terrible wailing lamentations were often heard there at night.

—G.T. Ridlon
Saco Valley Settlements and Families (1895)

wandering about the fertile intervales of the Israel River, and hearing moose-hunting stories.

The next morning they departed Dartmouth on the route south through the Western (Crawford) Notch

> a narrow defile between the Mountains, which rise perpendicularly on the eastern side, and on the other sides in an angle of 45°, forming a basin, in which is an open meadow, a most sublimely picturesque and romantic scene! This is the only practicable passage through the White Mountains.

The modern explorer departs Jefferson on Route 116 to Route 302, then proceeds south. A road, built upon "the proceeds of a confiscated estate," was under construction. The narrowest part of the defile was 22 feet. Here was the source of the Saco River, which the men planned to parallel on their return journey. Belknap, awed by what he saw, wrote:

> These beauties of Nature gave me inexpressible delight. The most romantic imagination here finds itself surprized and stagnated! Every thing which it had formed an idea of as sublime and beautiful is here realized. Stupendous mountains, hanging rocks, chrystal streams, verdant woods, the cascade above, the torrent below, all conspire to amaze, to delight, to soothe, to enrapture; in short, to fill the mind with such ideas as every lover of Nature, and every devout worshipper of its Author, would wish to have.

"It was with regret, Belknap wrote, "that I left this place and descended toward the south." The Saco is "rapid, and full of falls." Immense heights of rocks surrounded them.

> These, when incrusted with ice, being open toward the S. and W., reflect the moon and starbeams in the night, and are sufficient to give rise to the fiction of *carbuncles*, which the Native Americans and their captives used to report, and which have swelled into marvellous and incredible stories among the vulgar.

The locals as well believed that these mountains were "possessed by genii, or invisible beings, and therefore never ventured to ascend them." At Conway, for example,

> the good women were glad there were three clergymen in the company, because they hoped we

should lay the spirits" (this was their own expression). Our pilot, Captain Evans, who was a man of humour, assured them, at our return, that we had done it.

The circumference of the mountains, they judged, was about seventy miles. They guessed the number of summits to be ten, but confessed that it was "impossible to tell the exact number, unless we should make an aerial voyage, in a balloon." Here was the source of the great rivers of northern New England. *"If the roads were clear on the back of the Mountains, you might in the same day drink of waters of Saco, Amariscogin [Androscoggin], and Connecticut."*

The expedition split up at Conway; Belknap and his friend Daniel Little accompanied Captain Evans to his home at Fryeburg, the site of the infamous battle in 1725 between the Massachusetts militia, led by Captain John Lovewell, and the local Pequawket. The last day of the journey, Belknap returned through Maine to New Hampshire in

> company with a man from Saco, going in pursuit of his wife, who had run away with a company of Shakers, taking with her a borrowed horse, and 25 dollars out of her husband's desk, in his absence. The poor man, if he cannot find her, must lose his *money*, and pay for the *horse*, which some men would be glad to do for the sake of getting rid of such a *wife*.

The scientists had hoped to judge the height of the Great Mountain, but with bad weather conditions and uncertain calculations, they could only guess. Belknap thought it over nine thousand feet. But he knew how "deceptive" mountainous territory can be to an inexperienced observer. What was most significant about the journey, Belknap told his friend Ebenezer Hazard, was not what the "sons of science" saw, but what they did *not see*.

The culture of early New England and the legends of the White Mountains were inseparable. Here was the great hypothetical treasure-trove of New England, where fabulous crystals and gems shimmered and glowed, and treasure of gold and silver, or more modestly, limestone and lead, could be found a spade's depth away. Here the doomed rangers of Rogers' company abandoned to the mountain's angry spirits their cursed booty, the silver statue

The Battle of Lovewell's Pond

There were many ballads written commemorating Captain John Lovewell and his men who lost their lives at Fryeburg: the following is from the early 1800s, when the event was still legendary among New Englanders.

Lovewell's Fight by Thomas C. Upham

Ah! Where are the soldiers that fought here of yore?
The sod is upon them, they'll struggle no more,
The hatchet is fallen, the red man is low;
But near him reposes the arm of his foe.
The bugle is silent, the war-whoop is dead;
There's a murmur of waters and woods in their stead;
And the raven and owl chant a symphony drear,
From the dark-waving pines o'er the combatant's bier.
The light of the sun has just sunk in the wave,
And a long time ago sat the sun of the brave.
The waters complain, as they roll o'er the stones,
And the rank grass encircles a few scattered bones.
The names of the fallen the traveller leaves
Cut out with his knife in the bark of the trees,
But little avail his affectionate arts,
For the names of the fallen are graved in our hearts.
The voice of the hunter is loud on the breeze,
There's a dashing of waters, a rustling of trees,
But the jangling of armor hath all past away,
No gushing of life-blood is here seen to-day.
The eye that was sparkling, no longer is bright,
The arm of the mighty, death conquered its might,
The bosoms that once for their country beat high,
To those bosoms the sods of the valley are nigh.
Sleep, soldiers of merit, sleep, gallant of yore,
The hatchet is fallen, the struggle is o'er.
While the fir-tree is green and the wind rolls a wave,
The tear-drop shall brighten the turf of the brave.

—*Collections, Topographical, Historical, and Biographical, Relating*
Principally to New-Hampshire (1822)

of the Virgin Mary and silver candlesticks, having taken the treasure from the parish of the Catholic St. Francis Indians in the infamous raid on their village in 1759. Here were amazing summits of white moss and glimmering stone. Here were hobgoblins, the furious phantoms of the dead, a host of satanic forces, storming and booming and frightening countless generations of intervale dwellers. Here were stories of treachery, deception, and death.

Belknap, incredulous before the journey and doubly so afterward, sallied forth with a list of negative discoveries. "To begin as high as possible, then, I saw no silver mines," nor lead at least "no person knows where to find it," nor "limestone, which would have been of more service to the country than silver or gold mines"; no snakes nor any other serpentine creatures, physical or spiritual:

> we saw no hobgoblins, demons, nor cacodemons, no wandering ghosts, nor the least appearance of Hobamoke, though I suppose Dr. [Cotton] Mather would have said we had invaded his territories, being 'Prince of the Power of the Air'. Should you ask what is the cause of the white appearance of these Mountains, I would tell you in one word, snow, which lies on them, commonly, from September or October till July. There is no white moss, nor white flint, nor white rocks, which can give any such reflection as is caused by the snow.

Jeremy Belknap's accounts of the mountains ended up in various magazines and formed a cornerstone of volume three of his *History of New-Hampshire*, wherein he provided a name for the anonymous great summit that Evans, Cutler, Little, and the rest had ascended. Yet who precisely named Mount Washington is unknown. Perhaps it was Jeremy Belknap. Perhaps it was Manasseh Cutler, who was sufficiently intrigued with the mountain to journey to the summit again twenty years later in 1804. Or perhaps it was another frequent visitor to the mountains who saw them enough to know the character of the highest summit and how it resembled in its bearing and forceful presence General George Washington.

Mount Washington

The first intrepid mountaineers of Mount Washington did not have the option that today's traveler has to ascend the mountain by road. The carriage road was built in 1861 to accommodate the growing number of tourists coming to observe, paint, write about, and climb Mount Washington. The auto road, which begins at Pinkham Notch, covers eight miles and takes about thirty minutes to drive. It is not a walk in the park. There are very steep overhangs and breathtaking vistas. The steep grade puts quite a strain on the radiator, transmission, and brakes of the vehicle. Every mile there is a turnoff to rest the auto and driver. Upon reaching the summit the visitor can stroll about taking in the view, though the wind chill is fierce, even in summer. Fortunately one can retreat to the restaurant, museum, or store of the Mount Washington Observatory, a meteorological station staffed year round in some of the worst weather in the world.

From the summit of Mount Washington, the observer—with the aid of clear weather, binoculars, and a good imagination—can see most of the significant landmarks of New Hampshire. The surrounding mountain wilderness appears like a great rolling plain covered with the gray and green of summer's clouds and foliage; in winter it appears as a sea of gray and white. The distant Atlantic can be seen along with the state's major river systems. The frequent rains and melting snow atop Mount Washington engender tributaries of many of New England's great rivers. Waters of the east slope spawn the Peabody River, a tributary of the Androscoggin River of Maine, as well as the Ellis River, a tributary of the Saco. Maine's Saco River originates on the west slope of Mount Washington, after which it descends to the south and east through Conway, New Hampshire, and Fryeburg, Maine, before proceeding on its journey through Maine to the Atlantic. Mount Washington's west slope also engenders the waters of the Ammonoosuc, which flows west, joining the Connecticut River near Littleton.

These highland rivers have scarcely changed over the centuries. The explorer today, like early Americans and before them the Algonquians, can experience the ice cold water as it quickly descends to the lowest elevations, forming rapid, shallow streams. The descending streams build into rivers as the waters of frequent rainfall and melting snow fill the narrow, rocky river-beds. Mile by mile the river grows and its power intensifies. By the time the Saco reaches Bartlett, then Conway (on Routes 302 and 16), it has grown bold and powerful, yet still crystal clear and cold. Frequent floods over the centuries left behind layers of rich soil (that the locals called intervale) that drew eighteenth-century settlers from central and southern New Hampshire and Massachusetts to settle and farm the land. Andrew McMillan, for example, one of the first settlers of Conway, moved from

Who Was the First to Ascend Mount Washington?

For centuries it has been thought that Darby Field was the first to ascend Mount Washington in 1642, making him the first mountain climber in the history of North America. But Jeremy Belknap, the indefatigable researcher and New Hampshire's greatest historian, claimed that Field's journey was actually in 1632, and that he and Henry Josselyn of Maine accompanied Captain Walter Neal, who was the agent of the proprietors Ferdinando Gorges and John Mason. Belknap's unnamed source, which he transcribed at some point in the 1780s, described how Neal, Field, and Josselyn ascended Mount Washington, discovering on the summit the same pond Captain Wells would find frozen in 1725. This time it was thawed, yet cold, but delightful refreshment for the three adventurers, who waded in it, cooling their feet and washing their boots.

Concord (Penacook) in 1765 to open a store and tavern on the banks of the Saco. McMillan was a native of Ireland who immigrated to New Hampshire in the 1750s. As a young man, he fought alongside Robert Rogers. In 1759 Lieutenant McMillan led a detachment of men in the infamous attack on and retreat from the St. Francis Indian village. At Conway, McMillan's Tavern was the last important stop for explorers and hunters before they ascended the Saco or Ellis toward the daunting northern peaks.

Mount Washington Hotel, Bretton Woods

The Mount Washington Hotel at Bretton Woods near the Crawford Notch at the foot of Mount Washington was built in 1902. The idea of Joseph Stickney, who made his fortune in the railroad industry, the hotel was conceived as a playground for the rich. It is of the Spanish Renaissance style, impressive in its bright gaudiness, appearing as a castle in the mountains. The International Monetary Fund was established here in 1944 at a conference held by the victorious nations of World War II. The Mount Washington Hotel is a National Historic Landmark.

One frequent visitor to McMillan's during the several decades before, during, and after the American Revolution was Colonel Joseph Whipple, a Portsmouth merchant and land speculator who founded the town of Jefferson. Whipple initially called his settlement Dartmouth; he referred to it in letters as his "plantation." Whipple was the sole proprietor of this huge wilderness tract situated on the Israel River. He settled Dartmouth with servants (sharecroppers) who worked the land hoping one day to own it. Whipple's great house served as a makeshift fort and tavern. It lay on an old Native

The Mount Washington Hotel and the Ammonoosuc River

John Josselyn

John Josselyn, the English physician and botanist, came to New England at the invitation of his brother Henry. John made two voyages to New Engand, exploring the seacost, river valleys, and inland forests. On one occasion he and unnamed others journeyed to the White Mountains of New Hampshire. Josselyn left behind this description of Mount Washington:

The Country generally is Rocky and Mountanous, and extremely overgrown with wood, yet here and there beautified with large rich Valleys, wherein are Lakes ten, twenty, yea sixty miles in compass, out of which our great Rivers have their Beginnings.

Fourscore miles (upon a direct line) to the Northwest of Scarborow, a Ridge of Mountains run Northwest and Northeast an hundred Leagues, known by the name of the White Mountains, upon which lieth Snow all the year, and is a Land-mark twenty miles off at Sea. It is rising ground from the Sea shore to these Hills, and they are inaccessible but by the Gullies which the dissolved Snow hath made; in these Gullies grow Saven Bushes, which being taken hold of are a good help to the climbing Discoverer; upon the top of the highest of these Mountains is a large Level or Plain of a days journey over, whereon nothing grows but Moss; at the farther end of this Plain is another Hill called the Sugar-loaf, to outward appearance a rude heap of massie stones piled one upon another, and you may as you ascend stop from one stone to another, as it you were going up a pair of stairs, but winding still about the Hill till you come to the top, which will require half a days time, and yet it is not above a Mile, where there is also a Level of about an Acre of ground, with a pond of clear water in the midst of it; which you may hear run down, but how it ascends is a mystery. From this rocky Hill you may see the whole Country round about; it is far above the lower Clouds, and from hence we beheld a Vapour (like a great Pillar) drawn up by the Sun Beams out of a great Lake or Pond into the Air, where it was formed into a Cloud. The Country beyond these Hills Northward is daunting terrible, being full of rocky Hills, as thick as Mole-hills in a Meadow, and cloathed with infinite thick Woods.

—John Josselyn
New-Englands Rarities Discovered (1672)

American trail (today's Route 2) that connected the Androscoggin to the Connecticut River valley—hence the settlements of upper Maine to the settlements of upper New Hampshire and Vermont.

Joseph Whipple seems the logical choice for the honor of christening Mount Washington. He knew and was a supporter of George Washington. He was present when Washington made his northern tour of the United States soon after his inauguration as president, ending up in Portsmouth in November, 1789. Whipple traveled, sometimes yearly, through the Western Notch; Mount Washington soared high above to the north. The adulation that Washington enjoyed at Portsmouth almost necessitated that some permanent honor be bestowed upon the president. Perhaps it was Joseph Whipple who memorialized General Washington's name in granite for centuries to come.

CRAWFORD NOTCH

In 1785 the state of New Hampshire constructed the first passable road through the White Mountains at Crawford Notch. The Sokokis, Pequawket, and Penacook tribes had long passed through this crevice between peaks. During the wars with France from 1689 to 1763, Native Americans captured many British-American colonists and brought them through this Western Notch. The first white Americans to pass willingly through the Notch were rangers, such as Captain Thomas Wells and his men, and hunters, such as Timothy Nash of Lancaster, New Hampshire. Nash, who according to some stories was accompanied by Benjamin Sawyer, traversed the Notch in 1771, which inspired Governor John Wentworth to build a road through the Notch, paralleling the Saco upstream. After the War for Independence, road-building began in earnest, funded by the confiscated estate of the Tory William Stark, brother of the patriot John Stark. When John Evans led Jeremy Belknap, Manasseh Cutler, and Daniel Little through the Western Notch in 1784, road construction (today's Route 302) had been temporarily halted although already underway. An increasing number of travelers came through the Western Notch as the eighteenth century drew to a close.

By this time settlers had come to the Western Notch. The first were Eleazar and Hannah Rosebrook, who moved from the Upper Coos on the Connecticut to the wilderness just north of the Notch. The Rosebrooks lived a hardy existence in a rough log cabin. Travelers journeying through the Notch enjoyed their homely hospitality. Timothy Dwight, president of Yale College, scientist, and traveler, stayed with the Rosebrooks in 1797 on his journey through the White Mountains. George Shattuck, a botanist from Pennsylvania, ascended Mount Washington in 1807, using the Rosebrook cabin as his base to and from the summit. When the Harvard physician and botanist Jacob Bigelow journeyed through the Western Notch in 1816, he stayed briefly at the Rosebrooks. Bigelow was one of many nineteenth-century botanists who believed that the White Mountains and particularly Mount Washington offered floral specimens rarely seen elsewhere in New England.

As Bigelow followed the Saco through the Notch, of which the "gap is so narrow that space has with difficulty been obtained for the road," he was in awe by what he saw. "There is no part of the mountain more calculated to excite interest and wonder than the scenery of this natural gap. The crags and precipices on both sides rise at an angle of great steepness, forming a support of basement for the lofty and irregular ridges above. One of the most picturesque objects in our view was a cliff presenting a perpendicular face of great height and crowned at its inaccessible summit with a profusion of flowering shrubs," notably the lavender-colored rhodora (*Rhododendron canadense*), "in full flower."

Bigelow and his party paralleled the Saco on its descent to Conway, then proceeded up the Ellis River to Cutler's River, named for the botanist Manasseh Cutler. Following the river on its descent from Mount Washington, they ascended to the summit in about six and a half hours. Bigelow wrote:

> If the traveler could be transported at once to the top of this mountain, from the country below, he would no doubt be astonished and delighted at the magnitude of his elevation, at the extent and variety of the surrounding scenery, and above all, by the huge and desolate pile of rocks, extending to a great distance in

THREE: FOLLOWING THE PATHS OF RANGERS   97

Account of Crawford Notch

The Reverend Timothy Dwight, president of Yale College, scientist, writer, and historian, toured the White Mountains in 1797 and left behind this record:

> At the southeastern extremity of this farm, we had a new and very interesting retrospect of these mountains. Widest asunder where we stood, they gradually drew nearer until they closed in the northwest, exhibiting in the most lively manner the appearance of an avenue formed by mountains of vast height, and extending more than two miles in length. At the head of this avenue rose a pointed summit, white with naked rocks and overlooking every other.
>
> The Saco was already swollen to a millstream, and both itself and its tributary cascades enlivened our journey with their murmurs.
>
> When we had rode six miles farther, we came to another farm, occupied by a man whose name was Crawford. Here the mountains assumed the form of an immense amphitheater, elliptical in its figure, from twelve to fifteen miles in length, from two to four in breadth, and crowned with summits of vast height and amazing grandeur. Compared with this scene, all human works of this nature, that of Titus particularly, so splendidly described by Gibbon, are diminished into toys and gewgaws. Here more millions could sit than hundreds there, every one of whom might look down with a full view on the valley beneath.
>
> —Timothy Dwight
> *Travels, in New-England and New-York (1821–22)*

every direction beneath him, and appearing to insulate him from the rest of the world. But the length and fatigue of the approach, the time occupied in the ascent, the gradual manner in which the prospect has been unfolding itself, are circumstances which leave less novelty to be enjoyed at the summit, than at first view of the subject, would be expected.

At the summit Bigelow discovered a profusion of alpine plants that usually grow in arctic conditions. Here were the Labrador tea (*Rhododendron groenlandicum*), varied species of *Azalea*, the beautiful alpine bluet (*Houstonia caerulea*), goldthread (*Coptis trifolia*), *Diapensia*, and other wildflowers making their brief, brilliant appearance during the few snow-less summer months of the White Mountains.

Besides flora, Bigelow saw few birds, mammals, or reptiles, though he heard from local inhabitants of the frequency of moose, bear, wolves, and rattlesnakes. Regarding the latter, he wrote:

> We were told by the people in Bartlett and Conway, that the rattlesnake (*crotalus horridus*) infests the rocks and sides of the hills in great numbers, and that twenty of these reptiles had been killed in a day. They even approach dwelling houses, at the doors of which they have been killed. The inhabitants regard them with little apprehension, since they are represented as slow and clumsy in their motions, and as always giving notice on being approached, by a loud and long continued rattle, resembling very much the singing of a locust. We saw none of these serpents, and heard of no injury sustained by any one from their bite.

Botanists throughout New England and elsewhere followed in Bigelow's wake. Thomas Nuttall, an Englishman and Harvard College professor who journeyed across America on several occasions in search of unique and undiscovered flora, ascended Mount Washington from Pinkham Notch in August 1824. He filled his satchel with specimens and descended the slope of the Western Notch. There he found a place to stay for several days resting and arranging his new collection.

Nuttall's host was Ethan Allen Crawford, who had recently joined the Rosebrooks in their lonely existence at the Western Notch and had inherited the Rosebrook tavern. Crawford's father Abel Crawford also lived at the Notch, having married Hannah Rosebrook, daughter of Eleazar and Hannah Rosebrook. The lives and experiences of these stalwart pioneers is recounted by Lucy Crawford, wife of Ethan, in her *History of the White Mountains*,

Lucy Crawford's History

Along with her husband Ethan, Lucy Crawford was one of the first residents of what came to be called the Crawford Notch, which modern Route 302 traverses. An example of the challenges of her life on the frontier is found in chapter three of her History of the White Mountains, in which she described a fire that destroyed their cabin on the morning of July 18, 1818. It was also the morning of her son's birth. Lucy gave birth to the five pound boy, then lay quietly in her bed while Ethan went fishing to bring trout home for dinner. A Mrs. Boardman and her husband were traveling through the Notch and stopped at the Crawford cabin to refresh themselves. It was then that the fire broke out. Mrs. Boardman, though a stranger, took charge and came to the room where Lucy lay with her newborn baby, saying "Mrs. Crawford, do not be frightened, the house is on fire and cannot be saved; be quiet and keep still; you shall be taken care of; remember your life is of more value than all the property which is to be consumed." These words, Lucy recalled later: "calmed all her fears, and when left alone, she had the presence of mind to command herself without trembling. She arose and dressed herself, then went to the desk, which stood in the room, unlocked it, took out all the papers and other things of consequence from the drawers, and put them in a pine chest which stood near by; they asked Mr. Boardman to save it, which he did. She then went into another room and took out some drawers, and they were carried out and saved. She would have taken down the top of a brass clock, had it not been for Mrs. Boardman, who would, every time she saw her making exertions, admonish her by saying she was not aware of her critical situation, and as it hindered her by these arguments from doing much herself, Lucy gave up and was placed in an armchair and carried to the place" where Ethan, upon his return, found her. "The infant was the last thing taken from the burning ruins."

published in 1846.

The Crawfords hosted not only scientists but artists as well. The sublime beauty of the narrow valley amid massive peaks combined with the rustic and dangerous existence of the few families who resided at the Notch made for wonderful material for the idealic pastoral portraits that characterized nineteenth-century White

Mountain art. William Bartlett, Isaac Sprague, and Abel Bowen, among many others, made Crawford Notch one of the most frequent themes for American landscape painting.

ARTIST OF THE WORD

Many connoisseurs of the beauty of the White Mountains have attempted to describe the landscape in words, but there has never been such a poet of the mountains as Robert Frost. Born in San Francisco in 1874, Frost grew up in Salem, New Hampshire, and Lawrence, Massachusetts. His mother was Scottish and his father was a native of Kingston, New Hampshire; both parents were writers. William Prescott Frost, Jr., was a newspaperman; Isabelle Moodie Frost wrote children's literature. Besides a knack with words, however, Robert Frost also inherited his father's proclivity for erratic behavior, uncontrolled emotions, depression, and anxiety. Having worked at odd jobs while attending Lawrence High School and Harvard College, marrying Elinor White in 1895 and beginning a family, Frost's uncertainty and health problems compelled him to write poetry and take up farming. In 1890 he moved his family to Derry, New Hampshire, where he worked a thirty-acre farm and raised chickens. From 1906 to 1910 Frost taught at Pinkerton Academy in Derry. In 1911 he sold his farm and moved north to Plymouth, at the foot of the White Mountains, but after only a year of teaching he abruptly decided to move his family to England. Frost hoped that a life in England would invigorate his career as a poet, and he was right.

Frost's first collection of poems, *A Boy's Will*, was published in England in 1912. The poems represent his experiences living in New Hampshire in the preceding years. Many of the poems focus on autumn, a beautiful if anticipatory time in New Hampshire: leaves changing color and falling to the ground, frost on the fields, the increasingly cold north wind, the first snowfall, and the warnings of impending winter, as well as the gloom, cold, and death. The Frost reader can easily imagine the long walks he took in the forests surrounding his Derry farm. In much of his work, Frost contemplated the relationship between humans and the natural environment, which gives life and brings death. Frost experienced both in turn over

the course of four years from 1896 to 1900, during which he and Elinor underwent the joy of their son Elliott's birth and the overwhelming sorrow of his death to cholera. In "Now Close the Windows," he writes with his signature clarity, about mourning and the natural world:

> Now close the windows and hush all the fields:
> If the trees must, let them silently toss;
> No bird is singing now, and if there is,
> Be it my loss.

In 1914 before the start of World War I, Frost's second collection of poetry, *North of Boston*, was published. *North of Boston* creates such powerful, lyric images of New Hampshire that they became *the images* of New Hampshire in the public consciousness for years to come. Frost's New Hampshire is a place of simple pastoral beauty, where the ordinary seems remarkable and words lose their power to describe the wonder of nature and man's response—except through the pen of Robert Frost. Frost's verse, as in "Mending Wall," allows the reader to feel the presence of the past in each old stone wall that forms boundaries, separates property, and records lives in New Hampshire.

The success of *A Boy's Will* and *North of Boston* in England and their publication in America led to Frost's return to New Hampshire in 1915, when he purchased a farm at Franconia. Franconia is a picturesque mountain town situated just north of Franconia Notch, famous for the natural phenomenon known as an Old Man of the Mountain. This granite rock formation with the uncanny profile of a human face was known to the Penobscot Indians four hundred years ago. In 1805 white settlers discovered the Old Man, and for almost two hundred years visitors have journeyed through the Franconia Notch to view it. Unfortunately the ice and cold of numerous New Hampshire winters took a toll on the Old Man of the Mountain: It collapsed in May, 2003.

The traveler who follows Interstate 93 through the Notch finds himself surrounded by massive walls of granite and peaks jutting into the sky. West are the Kinsman mountains; east Mount Lafayette and Mount Lincoln. Clouds hang lazily amid the mountain slopes. Ice-cold mountain ponds such as Echo Lake and Profile Lake spawn streams flowing south and north. Echo Lake forms springs such as Lafayette and Gale. The latter becomes the Pemigewasset River. The Penacook once upon a time named the river "swift water." As it courses rapidly south through the Notch, it pounds at the rock and carves wonderful shapes with beautiful stony colors. Swirling water creates the Basin, a large pool of cold, clear, green water. Fog rises from this water meeting warm air. The forest is delightfully wet, unpleasantly humid, and an able host for mushrooms and wildflowers, such as the lavender hyacinth (*Camassia scilloides*) that grows in abundance. Such a place draws poets and writers.

The Frost farmhouse, built in 1859, is now a museum that is poised on a small forested eminence that looks south to the Franconia and Kinsman ranges. In the shadow of such peaks, Frost wrote, farmed, and rambled, following forest trails that traced the ageless paths of hunters, deer, moose, and bear. Here and there the trail forks, presenting the traveler with the choice of which path to take, Frost considered this fork akin to the choices life often presents. In *Mountain Interval*, poems written at Franconia, Frost relates through verse the paths that he chose.

Frost dedicated one poem, "Birches," to a familiar forest companion. The white birch (*Betula papyrifera*) is a deciduous tree amid so many pines. It should be small and indescript next to the towering white pine, yet the birch holds its own. The most beautiful white bark embraces the thin, delicate trunk. Upon a time, a young Frost climbed the thin birches to force them to bend one way or another until their leaves touched the ground. One gathers that even years later he could not resist such play. For miles around, bent birches decorate Frost's woods with arches through which one can walk.

Mountain Interval, like so many of Frost's books, evokes the simple beauty in the minutiae of nature. Frost treasured each season for its particular wonder. In summer the hilly slopes of the mountains were open to the inquisitive journeyer. Spring was the time when Frost became "Slave to a Springtime passion for the earth," as he puts it in his poem "Putting in the Sod." Autumn was when the scythe cut a broad swath in the field to gather the hay for winter.

Winter was the most anticipated time because of its cold and solitude. Frost was given to long walks in winters, but only in valleys. Frost's "Fire and Ice" conveys a sense of the brutality of the cold to be found in New Hampshire's mountains. In the poem's recounting of a debate between those who "say the world will end in fire" and those who say it will end in ice, Frost comes down, with characteristic Yankee understatement, on the side of ice, contending that "for destruction ice/Is also great/And would suffice."

Frost's collection of poems, *New Hampshire*, appeared in 1923. New Hampshire, according to his poem of the same name:

> Had one President (pronounce him Purse;
> And make the most of it for better or worse.
> He's your one chance to score against the state).

At the same time New Hampshire produced a counterpart to Franklin Pierce:

> Daniel Webster. He was all
> The Daniel Webster ever was or shall be.
> She had the Dartmouth needed to produce him.

And finally, New Hampshire is, Frost concludes:

> One of the two best states in the Union.
> Vermont's the other. And the two have been
> Yoke-fellows in the sap-yoke from of old
> In many Marches.

Frost's *New Hampshire* lauds the state's small mountains, small people, the unpretentious restfulness perfect for the farmer, dreamer, and poet, as well as famous native sons he would have liked to forget and a few he still cared to remember.

Canterbury Shaker Village, Canterbury

In 1792 the Shakers, Christian followers of Mother Ann Lee, came to Canterbury, New Hampshire. There they set up a communal living system of joint ownership, celibacy, equality among all, and worship that involved dancing and singing. The village today includes twenty-five historic structures amid a beautiful natural habitat of forests and ponds. The Shakers believed in hard work and piety. Like other Protestants they engaged in capitalism as well. Indeed the Shakers of nineteenth-century Canterbury became quite wealthy property owners. The last Shaker at Canterbury died in 1992. Today the village is a museum to preserve Shaker history and culture.

Above: Girls at the Canterbury Shaker Village do their gymnastic exercises; date unknown

4

THE CONNECTICUT VALLEY

Robert Frost referred to the Connecticut River as *that* shared by New Hampshire and Vermont; its source, he wrote, is "a trout hatchery near Canada." So one might think after journeying to the far north, where Vermont's width contrasts with New Hampshire's narrows, caused by the southwesterly flow of the Connecticut River. Frost's "trout hatchery" is in three stages, the source of the Connecticut being Third Connecticut Lake, Second Connecticut Lake, and First Connecticut Lake. Should one wonder that such wilderness ponds—delightfully cold, still in the morning, fog covered, and mirrors of the sky and trees— have such banal names, know that northern New Hampshire is known for its common sense, no-nonsense approach to things. If three ponds in sequence form the source of the Connecticut, why make their names prosaic? Such homely wisdom explains, perhaps, why the first people to cast their vote in presidential elections are the residents of Dixville Notch, a remote town in extreme northern New Hampshire.

The Upper Connecticut first drew settlers in the 1760s at the close of the French-Indian War. Veterans who had journeyed with Robert Rogers on expeditions against Canadian natives, and particularly those who considered the Connecticut their route to safety, revisited the valley during peacetime. The floods of millennia have formed an extremely fertile valley (intervale land) between Vermont and the New Hampshire hills. Men from Connecticut and Massachusetts ascended the river to farm the fertile soil and form towns. Many of the towns of the Upper Coos (Cohos) and Lower Coos (Cohos) have familiar Connecticut names, such as Lyme and Lebanon. Lancaster, founded in 1763 at the crossroads of Indian and hunting trails with the Connecticut, was the northernmost Connecticut River settlement until the founding of Colebrook in 1770, followed by the Indian Stream settlement around 1819.

Indian Stream descends from Canada just west of the Third Connecticut Lake and flows south a little over twenty miles to merge with the Connecticut north of Stewartstown on Route 3. Into this remote wilderness came hunter Luther Fuller in 1785. Fuller and others like him found the land a rich resource for beaver pelts, marten furs, and bear grease. They could live for days off a moose kill. Jeremiah Eames surveyed the land in 1789 in part to determine the precise boundary of New Hampshire and Canada. The wording of the Treaty of Paris that ended the American War for Independence in 1783 had been vague concerning the border with Canada. Hunters like Luther Fuller and land speculators such as Jonathan Eastman believed that the Indian Spring region was part of New Hampshire, not Canada. At the turn of the century and into the early 1800s, the Upper Connecticut at Indian Stream and the three Connecticut lakes attracted more hunters and speculators followed by settlers and their families. The state of New Hampshire attempted to assert its authority over the Indian Stream settlers in the 1820s, but the uncertainty of the boundary, hence the jurisdiction of the region, as well as the willfulness of the settlers resulted in the independent republic of Indian Stream in the 1830s. The republic had its own constitution and government, which incited a response from New Hampshire, asserting its claim to and jurisdiction over the land. The Indian Stream Republic called on Canada for protection, which led to a controversy between Canada and the United States over who ultimately had control over Indian Stream. Not until the Webster-Ashburton Treaty of 1842 was the controversy resolved. The Indian Stream Republic ceased to exist as it became a part of New Hampshire.

The controversy over Indian Stream was hardly a unique occurrence in New Hampshire history. The state was founded on land disputes. During the seventeenth and eighteenth centuries, John Mason and his heirs sought to own and control a large part of the colony based on the proprietorship granted to Captain Mason by King Charles I. The boundaries between New Hampshire and Massachusetts and New Hampshire and Maine (a district of Massachusetts until 1820), were under dispute for years.

Colonial governors such as Benning Wentworth, Governor of New Hampshire from 1741 to 1767, indulged in land speculation and rewarded political cronies with grants of land. Wentworth granted charters for thousands of acres in the Connecticut Valley and west to the Green Mountains. In fact what is today Vermont was in the mid-eighteenth century under contention by the colonies of New Hampshire, New York, and Massachusetts, the leaders of each believing that only they had rights to the lands of the Green Mountains. As some choice parcels of land were granted to proprietors multiple times, the region came to be known simply as the Grants. Into this confusing political situation came settlers up the Connecticut River looking to farm the rich land and to build communities.

Immigration to the Upper Connecticut Valley from 1763 to 1776 (following trails that became in time Interstate 91 in Vermont and Route 12 in New Hampshire) was sufficiently brisk to warrant the incorporation of several towns. Those on the eastern side of the Connecticut were constrained by the colony of New Hampshire to incorporate as New Hampshire towns and conform to New Hampshire jurisdiction. Yet the settlers felt detached and isolated from the rest of the colony. The White Mountains provided a sufficient natural barrier between central New Hampshire, drained by the Merrimack River, and western New Hampshire, drained by the Connecticut River, to confirm this isolation.

By the time the thirteen colonies declared their independence from Great Britain in 1776, settlers and land speculators wishing to establish the independent state of Vermont came together to form a coalition in a region of the Green Mountains west of the Connecticut Valley. Ethan Allen and the Green Mountain Boys provided a forceful, coercive presence in order to convince the slack-hearted of their design. These Vermonters invited the New Hampshire towns on the eastern banks of the Connecticut to join them in the creation of the proposed state. The vocal majority of the towns wished to join the Vermonters. By 1778, sixteen New Hampshire towns of the Connecticut Valley petitioned Vermont to allow them admittance. Vermont, of course, was agreeable. But New Hampshire, New York, even Massachusetts, had something to say about this bold proposal.

NEW CONNECTICUT

During the American War for Independence, Vermont and all those who tied their fortunes to this emerging independent republic were in a terribly confused situation. The Green Mountain Boys were independent to the core and wanted to ally themselves politically with whichever government could help them the most. They were inclined toward the new United States of America, but British authorities in Canada were actively courting them. The sixteen New Hampshire towns along the east side of the Connecticut River, also fiercely independent, thought that Vermont offered them the best hope of prosperity. But when in 1778 Vermont petitioned the United States Congress to consider Vermont statehood, including the sixteen Connecticut Valley towns, the Congress refused. The sixteen New Hampshire towns decided to take matters into their own hands.

In December 1778, delegates from the sixteen towns as well as from Vermont towns on the western shores of the Connecticut met in Cornish, New Hampshire, to proclaim themselves subject to their own independent jurisdiction. The government of New Connecticut was born.

The hopeful state of New Connecticut included towns of the Connecticut Valley ranging from Littleton in the north to Cornish in the south. The curious motorist today can explore what once was New Connecticut in a day with a good road map and a vigorous imagination. Route 10 parallels the Connecticut and follows a hilly, forested course from Littleton south to Lebanon, where the traveler can pick up Route 12A to Cornish. Littleton, a picturesque town north of Franconia Notch, preserves few vestiges from its time in New Connecticut. The Ammonoosuc winds through the town, powering even today the Littleton Grist Mill, a beautiful old clapboard building in its third century, still grinding wheat into flour. Traveling south, you come to the towns of Haverhill, Orford, and Lyme that fit well the image of old New Hampshire: large affluent farms, main streets lined with mansions built upon centuries of wealth, and roads winding through rural contentment. Lyme in particular has that postcard look about it.

Timber house, Lyme

Lebanon is the largest town that remains today from what was once New Connecticut. The Mascoma River flows into the Connecticut nearly opposite to where Vermont's White River joins the Connecticut. Like most of these Upper Valley towns, Lebanon—a mill town in the nineteenth century and before that a farm hamlet—was settled soon after the British victory over the French in the French-Indian War. After years of warfare during which the Connecticut was a thruway for raiders and pillagers, peace came to the valley. As Jeremy Belknap wrote in 1791:

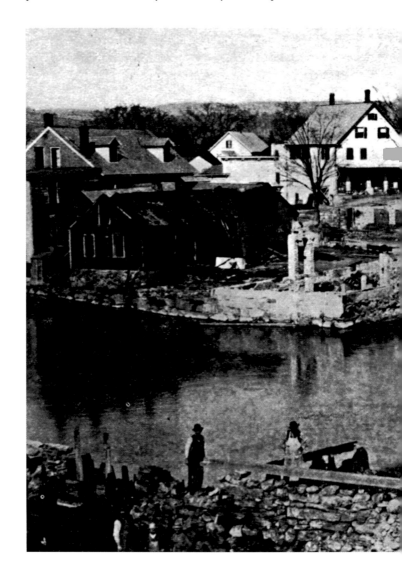

The passion for occupying new lands rose to a great height. These tracts were filled with emigrants from Massachusetts and Connecticut. Population and cultivation began to increase with a rapidity hitherto unknown; and from this time may be dated the flourishing state of New-Hampshire; which before had been circumscribed and stinted in its growth, by the continual danger of [the] enemy.

"May 10, 1887, looking east from where Everett Mill now stands," Lebanon

The Fort at Number 4, Charleston

Charlestown, New Hampshire, a small town located on Route 12 adjacent to the Connecticut River, was once known simply as No. 4. Massachusetts granted proprietorships for settling the land of what is today western New Hampshire (before 1741, Massachusetts considered the area part of its domain). There were four such proprietorships, the fourth being a fertile tract of land next to the Connecticut River. The first settlers arrived in the 1740s and built a small, fortified village. Upon the first hostilities in King George's War, Number 4 came under attack. Captain Phinehas Stevens was the commander of the fort during several years of skirmishes with Native Americans before peace brought an end to the war in 1748. The fort was almost lost to the enemy in April 1747. Jeremy Belknap told the story in his *History of New-Hampshire*:

> The enemy, finding that they were discovered, arose from their concealment and fired at the fort on all sides. The wind being high, they set fire to the fences and log-houses, till the fort was surrounded by flames. Capt. Stevens took the most prudent measures for his security; keeping every vessel full of water and digging trenches under the walls in several places; so that a man might creep through, and extinguish any fire, which might catch on the outside of the walls. The fire of the fences did not reach the fort; nor did the flaming arrows which they incessantly shot against it take effect. Having continued this mode of attack for two days... they prepared a wheel carriage, loaded with dry fagots, to be pushed before them, that they might set fire to the fort. Before they proceeded to this operation, they demanded a cessation of arms till the sun-rising, which was granted. In the morning... fifty men... demanded a parley, which was agreed to. A French officer, with a soldier and an Indian, then advanced; and proposed that the garrison bind up a quantity of provisions with their blankets, and having laid down their arms should be conducted prisoners to Montreal.

When Captain Stevens refused to back down, the enemy departed. Belknap concluded: "In this furious attack from a starving enemy, no lives were lost in the fort, and two men only were wounded. No men could have behaved with more intrepidity in the midst of such threatening danger."

The Fort at Number 4 fell out of use after the French-Indian War, until the Revolutionary War, when the fort was used as a supply depot and assembly point for soldiers. Today, a re-creation of the Fort at Number 4 is a living history museum open to the public. Costumed soldiers, goodwives, townsmen, and Native Americans provide a lively interpretation of life during King George's War, over 250 years ago.

Dartmouth College

One Upper Valley town, Hanover, refused to join its sixteen brethren in the temporary adventure of founding the state of New Connecticut. Hanover is noteworthy as the home of Dartmouth College. Eleazar Wheelock founded the College in 1770. Wheelock, a missionary to the Native Americans of Connecticut, decided to relocate his school to the Upper Connecticut Valley. With the help of English patrons, such as the Earl of Dartmouth, and a huge grant of land in New Hampshire made in 1769 by Governor John Wentworth, Wheelock located his school, renamed Dartmouth College, at Hanover. Of the move, Jeremy Belknap wrote:

> With these advantages and the prospect of a rapidly increasing neighborhood, in a fertile soil, on both sides of Connecticut river, Doctor Wheelock removed his family and school into the wilderness. At first, their accommodations were similar to those of other settlers, on new lands. They built huts of green logs, and lived in them, till a proper edifice could be erected. The number of scholars, at this time, was twenty-four; of which eighteen were white, and the rest Indians.

Jeremy Belknap attended the third commencement of the college in 1774, and he kept a journal that provides an intimate view of the new college.

Belknap journeyed from Dover to Concord, north to Plymouth, then west along what is today Route 25 and Route 25A through Wentworth to Orford. Now as then it is a forbidding, difficult land of dense forests covering mountains and valleys. The Appalachian Trail cuts through the region among Smarts Mountain, Mount Cube, and Piermont Mountain. Belknap covered sixteen miles on August 23, reaching Hanover, and Dartmouth College, at dinner-time.

Hanover and its college pleased Jeremy Belknap:

> The plain where the College stands is large and pleasant and the land good. The college is about seventy or eighty feet long and thirty broad, containing twenty chambers. The hall is a distinct building which also serves for a meeting house, and

the kitchen is in one end of it. The President's house stands on a rising ground east of the college, and to the north of this is the place proposed to build the new college near a quarry of grey stone which is intended for the materials of building. There is another quarry much larger about three-quarters of a mile distant. The tutors are Messrs. Woodward, Ripley, Wheelock and Smith; the two former are married to the President's daughters. Several tradesmen and taverners are settled round the College in good buildings, which gives the place the appearance of a village.

Such were the beginnings of the town of Hanover.

Dartmouth College Buildings, Dartmouth Row, 1880s

The Dartmouth "scholars" were independent and industrious; six of them lived in a grist mill that they operated between studies. The Native American scholars were similarly attentive to improving their lives. All of the students complained of the food, which was often moldy and rancid. President Wheelock considered any criticism to his college the meddling activities of the unrighteous. Even so, Belknap was impressed by "the improvements that have been made in four years." The library "is not large, but there are some very good books in it." Today this library on the college green, Baker Library, is a huge, imposing building with hundreds of thousands of volumes. It stands at the north end of the green; on the east side is a reconstruction of the most formidable building on campus, Dartmouth Hall, the construction of which began in 1784 under the supervision of Eleazar Wheelock's son and successor, the Reverend John Wheelock. Dartmouth Hall was completed in 1791, replacing the original college building that burned soon after Belknap's visit in 1774. Thereafter Dartmouth Hall was the center of the ever-growing campus. Although the first Dartmouth Hall burned in 1904, a replica was quickly constructed to replace it. Eleazar Wheelock, along with other Dartmouth notables, rests in an old cemetery just west of the college green.

Reverend Belknap's Itinerary, August 1774

Friday, August 26, Belknap set out in the fog along the Connecticut south to Lebanon. Lebanon today is a peaceful valley town surrounded by small peaks with which the church spires surrounding the town green sometimes compete. Larger mountains stand out of reach—Mount Ascutney in Vermont and Mount Cardigan near Canaan. The journey south along the Connecticut (today's Route 12A) was a "pleasant ride" in the forest through the small towns of Plainfield and Cornish. For the modern traveler, the latter town features a wonderful old covered bridge that spans the Connecticut as well as the home and gardens once belonging to Augustus St. Gaudens, the famous late nineteenth-century American sculptor. Belknap ended the day at Charlestown, once known simply as Number 4.

Arriving at Charlestown, Belknap commented that the town was a "pretty place" with "a wide, strait street and some good houses." The historian made no mention of Number 4, the famous fort that had for years served as the bastion of defense during the many wars between the English and the French. It was to Number 4 that Robert Rogers' Rangers—what was left of them—returned in the fall of 1759, having destroyed the Native American village at the St. Francis River then retreating through swamps and forests without food, pursued by the French and the rangers' own guilt.

Upon leaving Charlestown, Belknap rode south (today's Route 12) to Walpole, where he stopped to lunch and to

The Road through the Western Notch

This record of a petition addressed to the New Hampshire General Court to expend funds to built a road through the Western (Crawford) Notch found the General Court accommodating, it being wartime and roads essential for good communications:

Petition of Inhabitants relative to a Road from Conway: addressed to the General Court, 1780

Humbly Sheweth—

That wheras there is a Road cut and Partly Cleared and Bridged Leading from uper Coos to Conway So to Wolfbrough and Portsmouth which is through Considerable unapropriated Lands unlikely Soon to be Seteled at or near the white hills where if Some Expence was Properly Laid out would Shorten the travel from Connecticut River to the Seaports and Prevent the People at uper Coos being under Necessety to taking the tedious Route of Lower Coos of a Least forty or fifty miles farther   And wheras it is now a time of war and the People at uper Coos being the frontier of this State or the Continant in this Northern Quarter Exposed to alarms and attacks by the Enemy from Canada and having no Resorce for help or way of Retreat but by the way of Lower Coos (which think themselves Equaly Exposed) wherefore your Petitioners beg the Interposition of the Honbl Court that they would order the above Said Road way imeadiatly be made Passable with horses or Carraiges through Said unapropriated Lands at the Cost of the State and through the appropriated Lands at the Cost of owner that So Releif may Soner be had from the Interior to the Exterior Part of the State which will be of great importance to your Petitioners and of advantage to this State and the Publick in general and Your Petitioners as in Duty bound will Ever Pray

Northumberland May 25th 1780

Report of Committee relative to building a Road, 1780

State of New Hamps In the House of Representatives June 14th 1780. The Committee on the Petition from Northumberland Reported their Opinion that they Recommend the passing an Act appointing & authorizing some person or persons to seel at public Vendue One Thousand Acres of the Confiscated Land of William Stark adjoining to Conway & lay out the money arising by said Sale in making a good & passable Road through the Unappropriated Lands Mentioned by the Petitioners & make Return of such doing to the General Court as soon as may be which is Submitted in behalfe of the Committee, by E. Thompson,—Which Report being Read & Considered, Voted that it be Received and Accepted— Sent up for Concurrence

—John Langdon, Speaker

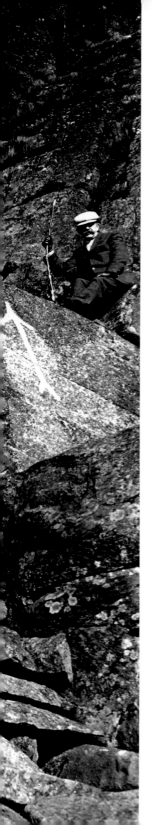

observe the most spectacular falls of the Connecticut River. A large rock stood in the middle, dividing the current into two arms. The combination of descending elevation, rocky obstructions, and water forced into narrow passages made for a delightful scene of white water. The rock had large cavities in it caused by centuries of rushing water. Fishermen hoping to land shad and salmon were in abundance. There was no bridge—yet. Within ten years the citizens of Walpole constructed a bridge that used the mid-stream rock as a buttress.

At Walpole the road turned southeast away from the Connecticut River. Likewise, today's Route 12 goes from Walpole to Keene. The Ashuelot River flows through Keene, and the Ashuelot River Park is one of the prime attractions of the city. When Belknap saw Keene in 1774, it was a small town on "a large plain surrounded with mountains." One mountain not too far distant from Keene is Mount Monadnock, "which is the highest mountain in these parts and the largest of a very long crooked range of mountains which go by the name of the Pack Monadnocks." The locals informed Belknap that the mountain roars before a storm and that winds might be calm on one side, yet violent on the other. Belknap had not the leisure to climb this mountain, like countless others have had in the intervening two centuries, but he later heard of the ascent of his friend James Winthrop in 1780. Winthrop used a barometer to

"The Last Climb 1911" Mount Monadnock

Cornish, New Hampshire

The small town of Cornish has much to offer travelers. The Cornish-Windsor Bridge, which spans the Connecticut River, is an astonishing relic from the past. Built in 1866, it is the longest covered bridge in the United States. The bridge, found off Route 12A, is supported midway by a granite buffer. The age of the bridge is revealed by a warning posted over its entrance: "Walk Your Horses Or Pay Two Dollars Fine." Cornish also boasts the Saint-Gaudens National Historical Site, which commemorates the life, work, studio, mansion, and property of Augustus Saint-Gaudens. The site includes many of his sculptures, as well as a nature trail, park, and beaver ponds. Saint-Gaudens brought together a host of artists and writers in the late 1800s, a group dubbed the Cornish Colony. Another famous resident of Cornish, Winston Churchill the novelist, lived at the Harlakenden House, which hosted guests such as President Woodrow Wilson; the house burned in 1923.

discover the height of the mountain at 3,254 feet, which was very accurate, off by only 100 feet.

The road from Keene to Peterborough was hilly and rocky, a difficult and fatiguing if beautiful ride. The stony land tried farmers' patience. For today's motorist driving Route 101 East, the rocks are a boon to travel, the ubiquitous stone walls making for a delightful compliment to the road. From Peterborough to Amherst, the road passed near Pack Monadnock, a smaller mountain than its cousin to the west. Countless streams watered the land, particularly the Souhegan River. The town of Wilton was built on the Souhegan. Belknap passed through Wilton quickly without having a chance to chat with the locals. Otherwise he would not have been silent about the recent "meetinghouse tragedy," in which five men were killed and scores injured during the construction of a new meetinghouse. The tragedy occurred less than a year earlier, in September 1773, when a support beam gave way as dozens of men were atop the unfinished rafters, frame, and scaffolding. Beyond Wilton, it was about a seventeen mile journey east to the Merrimack River, which

Belknap crossed at Lutwyche's Ferry, directly across the river from Litchfield.

From Litchfield Belknap traveled the route to Londonderry, Chester, and Epping. Today's Route 102 is an inexact replica, according to the course he took if not the sights he observed. The road is winding, a thoroughfare hemmed in by stone walls and arching pines. Cemeteries along the way, such as the old Chester Village Cemetery, founded in 1751, constantly recall the past. At towns such as Fremont, meetinghouses have withstood time to gather together generations of townspeople. Modern society has made inroads into these small New Hampshire towns, but such change is often difficult to see during cursory travels throughout the state.

5

THE MERRIMACK VALLEY

Jeremy Belknap used such journeys as his 1774 trip to Hanover to help him form impressions of the history of New Hampshire. In the early 1770s he decided to write an exhaustive narrative account of his adopted home. It took him over a decade to complete the first volume of his *History of New-Hampshire*; all three volumes were not finished until 1792. Belknap's work is a narrative of political, military, social, economic, and natural history. His *History* has never been surpassed, rarely equaled. For years writers, travelers, and historians have relied on Belknap's account of New Hampshire. One of these was Henry David Thoreau.

THOREAU'S JOURNEY

The Concord, Massachusetts, native Thoreau was a naturalist, writer, historian, and explorer. In 1839 he and his brother John set sail on the Concord River in a home-made fifteen-foot sailboat built "like a fisherman's dory." The Concord flows into the Merrimack River while still in Massachusetts. Thoreau claimed to have journeyed all along the Merrimack from its source at Lake Winnipesaukee following in the wake of the first explorers of this region, Jonathan Ince and John Sherman. Thoreau had also been to the source of the Pemigewasset, the first important river that feeds into the Merrimack at Franconia Notch. Besides the Pemigewasset, the Winnipesaukee, Baker, Souhegan, Piscataquoag, and Contoocook rivers feed the Merrimack. The Merrimack follows a southerly course through Concord, Manchester, and Nashua, then proceeds into Massachusetts where it abruptly turns to the east-north-east. The mouth of the Merrimack is at Newburyport. The sandy Plum Island bars the mouth from significant ocean traffic. As a result, the people of New Hampshire living in the Merrimack Valley turned to the river for fishing, inland trade, and manufacturing. Some of the most famous New England factory towns—Lowell and Lawrence, Massachusetts, and Manchester, New Hampshire—are built on the Merrimack. Thoreau discussed the impact of the Industrial Revolution on the Merrimack in *A Week on the Concord and Merrimack Rivers*, published in 1849. He wrote:

> Unfitted to some extent for the purposes of commerce by the sandbar at its mouth, see how this river was devoted from the first to the service of manufactures. Issuing from the iron region of Franconia, and flowing through still uncut forests, by inexhaustible ledges of granite, with Squam, and Winnepisiogee, and Newfound, and Massabesic lakes for its millponds, it falls over a succession of natural dams, where it has been offering its *privileges* in vain for ages, until at last the Yankee race came to *improve* them. Standing here at its mouth, look up its sparkling stream to its source,—a silver cascade which falls all the way from the White Mountains to the sea,—and behold a city on each successive plateau, a busy colony of human beaver around every fall. Not to mention Newburyport and Haverhill, see Lawrence, and Lowell, and Nashua, and Manchester, and Concord, gleaming one above the other. When at length it has escaped from under the last of the factories it has a level and unmolested passage to the sea, a mere *waste water*, as it were, bearing little with it but its fame; its pleasant course revealed by the morning fog which hands over it, and the sails of the few small vessels which transact the commerce of Haverhill and Newburyport.

The Thoreau brothers entered New Hampshire where the Merrimack drains the plentiful waters coursing through the towns of Pelham, Windham, Londonderry, and Nashua. When Thoreau saw Nashua it was "a manufacturing town" that received the waters of Salmon Brook and Nashua River. Mount Uncannunuc towered nearby to the northwest. As they made their way upriver,

Uncannunuc accompanied them, as it were, reminding Thoreau by its presence and its name that two centuries before this was Native American land—Naticook.

Passing Litchfield, the brothers encountered the first in a series of waterfalls. For the sake of trade, the state of New Hampshire had devised a series of locks and canals to facilitate river transport. The "lockmen" who lived at and worked the locks were loquacious, and their apparent Arcadian lifestyle fascinated Thoreau.

Roads paralleled the river, as does Route 3 today, hosting pedestrians, travelers on horseback, carts, and the occasional Concord Coach. Brooks and rivers fed the Merrimack: the Naticook around Thornton's Ferry, Baboosic Brook near Reed's Ferry, and Cohass Brook near Goffe's Falls. Massabesic Lake, then as today, was distant a few miles to the east. The land was rich in clay, and active brick-making operations were everywhere. The Piscataquog flowing in from the west signaled to the brothers that they neared Amoskeag Falls. The factories of the burgeoning town of Manchester used the force of the water to run the mills. It was a small town of 2000 that Thoreau saw—but every year the number of immigrants grew. The Penacooks, who once lived near here under their chief Wonolancet, had long abandoned the site to enterprising white settlers.

Belknap, who saw Amoskeag Falls before the founding of Manchester, described them as follows:

> Eight miles below Hookset, lies Amuskeag fall; it consists of three large pitches, one below the other, and the water is supposed to fall about eighty feet in the course of half a mile. The river here is so crooked, that the whole of the fall cannot be viewed at once; though the second pitch, which may be seen from the road, on the western side, appears truly majestic. In the middle of the upper part of the fall, is a high, rocky island, on some parts of which, are several holes, of various depths, made by the circular motion of small stones, impelled by the force of the descending water.

Today the view of the falls is obscured by the towering, ubiquitous red-brick mills built by the Amoskeag Manufacturing Company. The old buildings now host

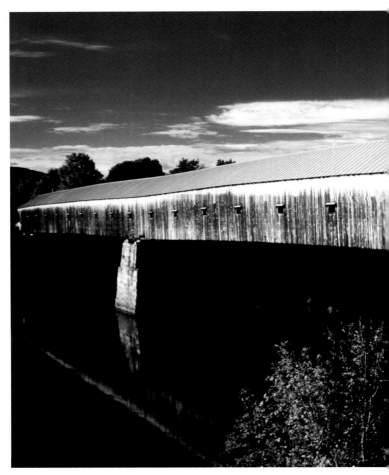

offices rather than factories. The drone of machines and sound of laborers, including the high-pitched voices of children at work, have succumbed to the noises of automobiles, computers, telephones, and shuffling of paper, and the faint murmurs of thousands of office workers.

Because of the falls and factories, Manchester grew quickly to become New Hampshire's largest city. It is a city of some culture that cannot escape its past as a factory town built on the labor of generations of impoverished factory workers.

When Thoreau saw the town in 1839, he guessed that its location and purpose heralded continued growth. Amoskeag Manufacturing, like so many of the early New England factories, employed young women who fit the ideal vision of a pastoral community of contented workers.

The Cornish-Windsor covered bridge connects the town of Cornish,
New Hampshire with Windsor, Vermont

Competition with other factories and cheap immigrant labor destroyed the pastoral imagery even if the company continued to employ it to consolidate a paternal hold over its employees. Laborers worked twelve hour days for little pay. The company provided housing and stores and docked wages accordingly. Many children worked, usually in unsafe, at times deadly conditions. The Progressive Movement of the early 1900s brought much needed reforms to limit the exploitation of factory workers. A general industrial decline throughout New England accompanied by labor unrest and unions resulted in the closing of the doors of Amoskeag Manufacturing in the 1930s.

MASSACHUSETTS PIONEERS

A century before the Thoreau brothers' leisurely excursion into New Hampshire, other Massachusetts adventurers ascended the Merrimack into New Hampshire. They came not for leisure but survival. Searching for new forests to clear and lands to farm, farmers and adventurers from Massachusetts were attracted to the rich fertile intervale lands of the upper Merrimack. Today the traveler on Interstate 93 north, where it parallels the Merrimack from Manchester to Concord, shadows the northward journey of these pioneers.

Jonathan Ince and John Sherman first blazed the trail in 1652, ascending the Merrimack to its source at Lake Winnepesaukee. Ince and Sherman traveled through lands dominated by the Penacook tribe and their chief Passaconaway. The Penacooks held a loose hegemony over other Algonquin tribes of the Piscataqua, Merrimack, and Connecticut valleys. Passaconaway was the dominant chief when the first English settlers arrived to the region in the 1620s and 1630s. He reputedly had vast powers at his disposal that he chose to rein in so to avoid conflict with what he considered to be a more powerful force. Legends abounded among Native Americans and whites about his ability to control the forces of nature, about his death and subsequent influence beyond the grave, holding sway over the spirit world atop Mount Washington.

But if Passaconaway was able to maintain peaceful if tentative relations with the English settlers, his successors Wanalancet and Kancamagus were not as successful, and the Penacooks slowly retreated north following the Pemigewasset River into the White Mountains and beyond. Their route would have taken them along today's Route 93 through Boscawen and Franklin to Plymouth. Today the town features the picturesque Plymouth State University. But to the forlorn Native American refugees, Plymouth would have meant nothing more than a place at the confluence of the Baker and Pemigewasset rivers. Some of the Penacook no doubt turned west following the Baker River upstream toward a ridge of hills that today forms a part of the White Mountain National Forest. As the men and women paralleled the shallow, cold Baker, they could spy the distant hills to the north that perhaps they eventually journeyed toward, passing under the shadow of the massive Mount Moosilauke (which the traveler can do today on Route 118—a beautiful and exciting drive).

The memory of the Penacook tribe is still retained by a town of that name, just north of Concord. Penacook is ironically best associated with the bloody exploits of Hannah Dustin, a native of Haverhill, Massachusetts, who having been captured by Native American raiders turned the tables on her captors and killed and scalped them.

SIGNS AND TIMES

Throughout the state, the New Hampshire Division of Historical Resources has posted over 150 historical markers to commemorate important events, places, and people. Marker no. 49 marks the general area where Hannah Dustin was confined before her escape. Indeed the Merrimack Valley, in particular Concord, the capitol of New Hampshire, has its fair share of historical markers. Concord monuments that commemorate New Hampshire's political past include the Pierce Manse, the home of Franklin Pierce, fourteenth President of the United States from 1853 to 1857. The inquisitive tourist can also see the Governor's Residence, formerly the dwelling of Styles Bridges, New Hampshire Governor and Senator; Bridges was a major political force in American politics during the 1950s. Nearby is the Christa McAuliffe Planetarium, named in honor of the teacher who perished

Museum of New Hampshire History, Concord

The Museum of New Hampshire History is connected to the New Hampshire Historical Society. The museum holds manuscript documents and artwork covering New Hampshire's 400 years. For example the Concord Coach, built by the Abbot-Downing Company in the early 1800s, is on display at the Museum. The Museum sponsors educational activities for New Hampshirans and visitors of all ages. Museum exhibitions have included spotlights on the art of Celia Thaxter, the New Hampshire primary, the life of Mary Baker Eddy, and the life of Franklin Pierce.

in the space shuttle *Challenger* disaster in 1986. Another Concord resident was Mary Baker Eddy, the founder of the Church of Christ, Scientist, who lived in Concord from 1892 to 1908. Concord was once the home of the eccentric Benjamin Thompson, who was a brilliant philosopher and scientist but a Tory as well. Thompson left New Hampshire because of the War for Independence, traveled to Britain then to Europe, where he became a Prussian nobleman. He adopted the title Count Rumford in commemoration of his years in Concord before the Revolution, when the town was called Rumford. The name Concord was adopted to symbolize an era of peace that came to central New Hampshire after the end of the French-Indian War and the end (for a time) of attacks from Native American raiders. Rumford had also been involved in extensive controversy with residents of nearby Bow over land grants given for the same land by both the governments of New Hampshire and Massachusetts. Upon a decision from the British Crown in favor of the residents of Bow, the losers of Rumford went in search of other lands, which led to the settlement of the upper Saco Valley, and towns such as Conway, New Hampshire, and Fryeburg, Maine. Concord, devoted to peace, would in time become the capitol of New Hampshire in 1816.

Marker no. 66 at the state capitol informs the visitor that the building is, like so many other public buildings in New Hampshire, made of native granite; it was completed in 1819 and still hosts the sessions of the New Hampshire state legislature. The gold dome of the Capitol glistens in the sunlight. North of the Capitol once stood the North Meetinghouse, where New Hampshire delegates to the Constitutional Convention, meeting in late 1787 and early 1788, ratified the United States Constitution. Article 7 of the Constitution declared that ratification of the Constitution occured when nine of the original thirteen states voted for it. When New Hampshire delegates voted for the Constitution in February 1788, New Hampshire became the ninth and deciding state.

Politics in New Hampshire have always been governed by tradition. The state motto (found on the license plate) claims that New Hampshirans "Live Free or Die." Such were the words of John Stark, one of New Hampshire's

The Capitol Building, Concord
Photo courtesy Juliana Spear

most famous patriots. John Stark of Londonderry, New Hampshire, was a frontiersman and hero of the American Revolution. As early as 1752, while hunting on the Baker River with his brother William, he was captured by Native American raiders and taken to Canada, where he was later ransomed. Several years later during the French-Indian War, he was a lieutenant leading rangers under the command of Major Robert Rogers. Stark was a colonel and then a general during the War for Independence. He saw action in battles at Charlestown, New Hampshire, and Bennington, Vermont. At the latter in August 1777, Stark and his New Hampshire militiamen defeated British troops in a pitched battle, keeping southern Vermont, western New Hampshire, and western Massachusetts secure from the enemy. This was the most famous victory by a son of New Hampshire during the American Revolution.

New Hampshire's focus on the freedom of the individual and the active participation of the people in local, state, and national politics is revealed in the ubiquitous town hall. Here, situated across from the common and around the corner from the Congregational parish, beats the heart of New Hampshire government. Hidden deep within the dusty caverns of town cellars are the records of town meetings, selectmen's reports, tax lists, and poor lists: These chronicle the power of town government over the centuries. Much of this tradition sailed across the Atlantic with the likes of David Thomson and Edward Hilton. Poor relief is a good example. English local government began providing alms and work for poor parishioners as early as the sixteenth century. As time passed, local poor relief, centralized and stimulated by the English Crown, became more sophisticated and complex. But legal codes soon became too repetitive, signifying the failure of the system. Nevertheless New England towns, inherently conservative, retained the English poor relief system. Poor relief in colonial New Hampshire was centered at Portsmouth. The institutionalization of the poor during the eighteenth century changed from a simple almshouse to a more structured and demanding workhouse, then finally the house of correction, which was little more than a prison.

But while poor relief altered with time, town leadership remained constant. Each New Hampshire town had an assembly of male citizens who passed the laws and elected town officials and authorized their power. Selectmen ran day to day affairs. Constables provided limited law enforcement and collected taxes. Auditors checked town accounts. Fence-viewers determined property boundaries. Hog-reeves corralled errant swine in the town pen.

New Hampshire Politics

New Hampshire has always held a leading if untraditional, role in American politics. That Franklin Pierce became President of the United States from 1853 to 1857 is evidence of New Hampshirans' independence of mind. Pierce was son of New Hampshire Governor Benjamin Pierce. The Pierce Family Homestead, built by his father the same year that Franklin was born, still stands at Hillsboro. During the 1830s and 1840s, the younger Pierce served in the New Hampshire legislature followed by stints in the United States House of Representatives and Senate. He fought in the Mexican War—indeed he was exceptional among New Englanders for supporting the war. Pierce had the unenviable role of being a Democrat in Federalist/ Whig/Republican New Hampshire. The Democratic party had southern slave interests and supported such unpopular policies (in New England) as the Fugitive Slave Act, states' rights, and the legitimacy of slavery. Standing for such beliefs and policies, Franklin Pierce defeated the Whig candidate General Winfield Scott in 1852 to garner the presidency. But his pro-slavery position helped lead to a split among the Democrats, which acerbated the growing sectionalism between the North and the South. Pierce lost the support of his party and was not re-nominated in 1856. Pierce was good friends with Nathaniel Hawthorne, who wrote a biography to help get his friend elected in 1852.

New Hampshire, of course, also hosts the first presidential primary. Why New Hampshire? It has to do with that unwavering independence the people of New Hampshire have exhibited over the course of four hundred years. As they developed during the nineteenth century, American politics focused increasingly on the influence of

local, state, and national political machines in electing hand-picked choices. State legislatures rather than the people elected U. S. senators to office. The political machines of the Republicans and Democrats geared up every four years to select candidates at political conventions. During the Progressive Era from 1900 to 1920, democratizing changes came to American politics: The Constitution was amended to provide for the direct election of Senators and women's suffrage. Further evidence of America's move toward a more representative democracy occurred when New Hampshire (along with two other states) established the first presidential primary in 1916. The goal of the primary was to get voters to participate directly in selecting party candidates to run for the presidency. The idea caught on and spread to other states. Today the New Hampshire primary is considered to be the first step upon which a presidential candidate must focus attention in the long process of electing the president of the United States.

New Hampshire has experienced several capitols over the course of its long existence. Portsmouth was the provincial capitol of New Hampshire, but with the coming

Birthplace of Franklin Pierce, Hillsboro
Photographs courtesy Juliana Spear

BUILT IN 1804 BY BENJAMIN PIERCE
OFFICER IN THE REVOLUTIONARY WAR
ND GOVERNOR OF NEW HAMPSHIRE IN 1827—182!
BIRTHPLACE OF HIS SON FRANKLIN PIERCE
FOURTEENTH PRESIDENT OF
THE UNITED STATES

RESTORED AND GIVEN TO THE
STATE OF NEW HAMPSHIRE IN 1925
AS A MEMORIAL TO
MAJOR FREDERICK A. KENDALL
U. S. ARMY 1861——1884 AND
VIRGINIA HUTCHINSON KENDALL
BY THEIR SON
APTAIN HAYWARD KENDALL, U.S. ARMY 1917—191!

of the Revolution, the General Court (legislature) moved up the Piscataqua and the Great Bay to Exeter on the Squamscott River. It was at Exeter that New Hampshire declared independence from England in January 1776. Here the state constitution was adopted and the first chief executives, presidents, of New Hampshire, signed legislation and executed the laws of government. Concord, building on its central location and important role in hosting the convention that ratified the Constitution in 1787-1788, eventually secured the privilege to host New Hampshire's government, becoming the capitol in 1816.

Governors of the independent state of New Hampshire were styled *presidents* until 1793. The first president of New Hampshire holding office from 1776 to 1784, was Meshech Weare of Hampton, whom Belknap praised for his honesty, dignity, and—unique in politics—*poverty*. Similar in character but not in fortune was John Langdon of Portsmouth, the leading New Hampshire conservative who was a signer of the Declaration of Independence and a New Hampshire delegate to the Constitutional Convention in 1787. Langdon lived in a mansion (kept spotless and elegant by numerous slaves and servants) in Portsmouth that still stands. Langdon served several terms as governor (and president) of the state from 1784 to 1812.

John Sullivan, veteran of the war and firm hand in New Hampshire politics, was elected president of New Hampshire in 1784 and again in 1789. It was Sullivan who put down a rebellion being fomented in Exeter in 1786 to take control of the state government. Liberal and lower class New Hampshirans were upset that there was a scarcity of gold and silver specie, and that in the difficult times of the post-revolutionary 1780s farmers were increasingly in debt and losing their land to rich speculators. Those wanting economic change demanded a reduction in, even forgiveness of, debts as well as an increase to the money in circulation by means of the government printing paper money. Their hope was that prices for farm goods would rise hence helping farmers hold onto their lands. The state government at Exeter was, however, dominated by conservatives who feared the rise in power of the lower classes. They refused to increase the circulation of currency. The liberal party decided to take matters into their own hands, and marched

American Independence Museum, Exeter

The American Independence Museum is a complex of several historical landmarks at Exeter on the Squamscot River. Exeter was the Revolutionary capitol of New Hampshire, where the Declaration of Independence was first read to New Hampshirans in July 1776. Exeter also held the initial convention to consider the ratification of the U. S. Constitution in 1787. The Ladd-Gilman house was built in the early 1700s by Nathaniel Ladd and was later occupied by merchant Nicholas Gilman. The Ladd-Gilman house served as the state treasury for a short time, and as a governor's mansion. The house was purchased early in the twentieth century by the Society of the Cincinnati. The Society also purchased the Folsom Tavern, which was opened in 1775 by Samuel Folsom.

on Exeter with muskets armed and sabers drawn. The rebellion quickly dissolved when General Sullivan led organized militia to break up the mob. This New Hampshire rebellion presaged the more famous Shays's Rebellion of 1787 in Massachusetts.

Such disorder convinced conservative statesmen such as John Langdon and George Washington that a new government, that of the Constitution, should be established to promote order. In fact upon the installation of Washington as the first president of the United States in 1789, he journeyed north to New England, visiting New Hampshire in November. Washington discovered that the Constitution provided for an orderly government and society in New Hampshire. Another president of New Hampshire, Dr. Josiah Bartlett, was the fourth man to serve as chief executive of the state, from 1790 to 1794. Bartlett was a member of the Continental Congress that produced the Declaration of Independence in 1776 and the Articles of Confederation in 1777. He served in Congress for several years during the war, and was also Chief Justice of New Hampshire. He died in 1795.

JOSIAH AND MARY BARTLETT OF KINGSTON

Traveling about the Merrimack Valley, the wayfarer finds in exploring the intricate network of state highways and local roads the ubiquitous presence of the past, notwithstanding the demands of modern society. This is particularly true in the region of southeastern New Hampshire among the towns of Kingston, East Kingston, Kensington, Brentwood, Hampstead, Danville, and Newton. The region is a low-lying land of small hills, tall pines, small rivers and smaller brooks, ponds, and bogs. The latter is the haven for the mosquito, the bane of the north woods. Locals designate as ponds the small lakes that feed and are fed by the plentiful brooks and rivers. Great Pond in Kingston, for example, is fed by Powwow River, which also forms Powwow Pond in Newton. Halfmoon Pond is just west of Great Pond, and Long Pond in Danville is just west of Halfmoon. These ponds contribute their waters to the Powwow River, which continues on its southeasterly course through South Hampton to Massachusetts and the Merrimack River. North of Kingston, Little River and Exeter River flow through Brentwood. Nearby is a large cedar swamp. The Exeter River flows into the town of Exeter to merge with the Squamscott.

American colonists settled this region in the late 1600s; many immigrated from Massachusetts, which is but a dozen miles to the south. Today's Route 125 reveals the route of wayfarers of three centuries ago. This path into the forest, surrounded by pines and birches, outcrops of granite and small ponds and brooks, has been transformed in recent years because of the requirements of modern society. The state of New Hampshire tries to attract businesses to its very conservative tax environment: no sales tax, no personal income tax. Towns near the Massachusetts border therefore draw residents of that state to shop. As a result in Plaistow and Kingston, just north of Haverhill, Massachusetts, the Route 125 corridor has become host to endless strip malls, automobile and recreational vehicle dealerships, and gift and antique shops. The small town character of Plaistow and Kingston has been seriously undermined.

To leave Route 125 for more narrow, less traveled lanes can still be refreshing. Kingston Village, for instance, still maintains the traditional town green surrounded by ancient homes and businesses. The 1686 House hosts a restaurant amid its colonial decor. The Kingston Library is a structure straight out of the Victorian Age. One can find old graveyards with toppled granite stones, such as Happy Hollow, a small yard in South Kingston next to Route 125. The First Congregational Church looks like the model for all colonial American churches: white clapboard, black shutters. A most imposing house in the center of town is the Bartlett Home, the onetime residence of Dr. Josiah and Mary Bartlett.

The correspondence between Josiah and his wife Mary Bartlett is revealing of eighteenth-century rural values amid a maturing political and social environment. Josiah, as a delegate from New Hampshire to Congress, departed for Philadelphia in September 1775, leaving Mary to care for the farm and their young children. These included Mary, Lois, and Hannah, the latter of whom was born while Josiah was away a second time in Philadelphia during the winter of 1776. Josiah had to endure being inoculated for the smallpox, the hotter weather at Philadelphia compared to Kingston, and the scarcity of good New England apple cider. Josiah also missed the rural existence of his home state, the slow daily life on a farm in Kingston, New Hampshire. In October 1775 Josiah wrote to Mary of his work on the problems of war and government and of the smallpox, so prevalent in Philadelphia:

> I have been Inoculated for the Small Pox and am almost Got well of it[.] I had it very favorable not above 20 Pock or thereabout Tho I was Confined by the fever to the House 5 or 6 Days[.] It is 4 weeks this Day Since I left Kingstown and have not heard from you Since I Saw you[.] I want very much to hear from you Tho I know you have the same almighty preserver in my absences—as soon as I Can you may be sure I Shall Return with great pleasure[.] The Living in So Grand a City without the pleasure of a free Country air is not very agreeable to me.

Mary responded to such letters, sending detailed accounts of family and community matters. She kept Josiah up to date on deaths, particularly of children, in their parish, the progress of the harvest and condition of the maize and apple

Merrimack Valley Winter, 1746

Rev. Timothy Walker served as the Concord, New Hampshire, minister for fifty-two years from 1730 to 1782. During this time Concord (originally called Penacook) was a frontier outpost continually harassed by Native American attacks, as Walker's diary of 1746 makes clear:

Woodwell's Garrison was taken April 22
Thomas Cook killed May ye 9.
Richard Blanchard scalped June 11.
Bishop was captivated June 25.
Jona Bradley killed Aug: 11.
Easterbrook killed Novr 10.
Killed, 8. Captivated, 12. Died of his wounds, 1.

Hi daily entries show a quieter existence, as this portion of his winter entries show:

January.
1, D. Very cold. Remained at Woburn.
2, D. At night went and lodged at Brother Walkers.
3, D. Sat out homeward. Lodged at Mr. Flaggs.
4, D. Arrived home.
5, D. Preached all day at home.
6, D. Visited over ye River.
7, D. Moderate weather.
8, D. Ditto.
9, D. Snowed and then turned to rain. Visited with Mr. Stevens over ye River.
10, D. Cleared up very cold. Capt. Goffe dined at our house.
11, D. A very cold morning Went up to Contoocook.
12, D. Preached all day there. Mr. Page preached here. Returned home at night.
15, D. Capt. Eastman and wife dined at our house. Remainder of ye week tarried at home. This week has been very warm.
19, D. Preached all day at home.
20, D. Visited Mr. A. Whittemore being sick of fever.
22, D. Visited at Deacon Merrill's.
25, D. A warm snow. This week; also has been very warm.

26, D. Preached all day at home. Cleared up very blustering. Ye new snow being about mid leg deep drifted very much.

27, D. Warm again

27, D. Moderate ye rest of this Week.

February.

1, D. A. M. Snowed. Mr. Stevens came and lodged at our house.

2, D. He preached here and baptized Abraham, ye son of Abm Colby; Evenr. ye son of Sampson Colby, and Abigail ye daughter of James Abbot Junior. I Preached at Contoocook.

3, D. At night it hail a great deal.

4, D. Visited at Mr. Lovejoys. Ye rest of ye week very warm.

8, D. It seemed to thicken up for a storm of rain but cleared away again.

9, D. Preached all day at home, and baptized Isaac ye son of Benjn Abbot and Sarah ye daughter of Joseph Pudney.

10, D. Eben Hall came to live with me. We sledded wood.

11, D. Ditto.

12, D. At night Col. Rolfe returned from Newbury. It was a cold night for this moderate winter.

13, D. Col. Rolfe dined at our house.

14, D. Warm again. Snowed a little.

15, D. Ditto.

16, D. Preached all day at home.

17, D. Fair weather. Received a letter from Woburn.

19, D. Visited with Col. Rolfe over ye River. At night he lodged at our house. N. B. From the 8 instant to ye 20 inclusive got home about 30 loads of wood for my years stock.

21, D. A very cold, blustering day.

22, D. Ye weather moderated. Looked like rain but turned to a spitting snow.

23, D. Preached all day at home, and baptized Ezekiel ye son of Tim. Walker Junior.

24, D. Extraordinary cold for ye season. Visited at Col. Rolfe's. Pd. Mr. Simonds for my barrel of cyder.

25, D. Cold. Carried my wife up to Mr. Lovejoy's a visiting.

—from "The Diaries of the Rev. Timothy Walker"
New Hampshire Historical Society

Alan Shepard (1923-1998)

Alan Shepard, a native of East Derry, New Hampshire, attended school at Pinkerton Academy in Derry. He graduated from the United States Naval Academy and fought in World War II. After the war he became a test pilot and in 1959 a Mercury astronaut. In May 1961 Shepard became the first American in space flying a small space capsule for fifteen minutes. Ten years later Shepard was aboard Apollo 14, which landed on the Moon in February 1971. Shepard took time to try a golf swing on the surface of the Moon. He died of leukemia in 1998.

trees, and specifics on the weather, especially rainfall and snow amounts. Josiah gave Mary instructions on the farm work, which she passed on to the hired hands. Mary kept up her spirits during Josiah's long absence by reassuring herself of God's watchful care. When winter approached with no sign of Josiah's return, Mary, several months pregnant with their third daughter and knowing the hazards of childbirth, urged him to return home, writing:

Their [sic] has been no funeral in this Parish Since them I mentioned you but in the East [Kingston] Parish Mrs tilton wife of Captn tilton buried her only Daughter Last wednesday; a bout four or five years old[.] She died with the feaver and Canker[.] He is Gone to Canada heavy news to him when he Comes to hear of it…. The people among us is [sic] very hurried Gitting [sic] in the English harvest; I believe they will Chiefly finish this week; we have cut all our Grain; Something Late Gitting in hay; we have not half Done as the Grass Grew very fast of late…. Pray Do come home before Cold weather as You Know my Circumstances will be Difficult in the winter If I am alive.

Josiah did come home during the winter, and was present at the birth of his daughter; unfortunately she died soon after. Asked to journey to Philadelphia to serve in Congress during the 1777 session, Josiah declined, citing fatigue, knowing that Mary and the children needed him more.

The pastoral feeling of New Hampshire towns has been one of the state's many attractions during the past century, particularly as some of the foundations for the state's economy, such as textile and shoe mills, the lumber industry, and mining, have dwindled. During the nineteenth century, people from Massa-chusetts, particularly the rich of Boston and its vicinity, began to travel to New Hampshire for a country get-away. Along the seacoast and in the mountains, towns such as Hampton and North Conway capitalized on the new tourist industry, which was the result of American urbanization. Writers such as Nathaniel Hawthorne and Henry David Thoreau longed for the pre-industrial, rural existence of the Massachusetts of their youth, which seemed to be vanishing even then. They sought pristine nature in New Hampshire. Today, for the same reason, so many visitors come to New Hampshire that the state is often overburdened by traffic jams, development, and a tourist industry that often borders on a carnival atmosphere.

Epilogue: Country Pond

Notwithstanding the changing landscape and increasing demands on the resources of the state, the on-the-road explorer can still find out-of-the way spots that recall the distant colonial past. Such a place is Country Pond, located in South Kingston off the busy Route 125. The narrow, dark, forested road that leads to the pond winds about a swampy landscape in which waterlogged soil can no longer sustain the towering white pines that lean in different angles, parts of their moss-covered trunks and roots protruding into the open air. The road narrows, then ascends, a small hill to a point at which Country Pond spreads out before the observer.

Country Pond is about a mile wide from shore to shore. A great peninsula separates two arms of the pond. A forested, abandoned island sits in the middle, inviting the imaginative to wonder what is within. Two brooks, Bartlett and Colby, feed the pond, which itself is a source of the Powwow River. The water is clear enough, especially in the morning before the rising of the wind, when the pond's mirror surface seems an untouched image harking back to the Creation. Fog frequently blankets the pond at morning. By the time the sun is high, the fog dissipates and the mirror vanishes, leaving the wind to stir up the water and the muddy bottom. The pond hosts a variety of fish, especially bass, perch, sunfish, bluegill, and the smooth-skinned pickerel. The pickerel loves weeds and lily pads, of which Country Pond has plenty. The muddy pond bed is also host to large numbers of fresh-water clams. The air is moist and humid, a paradise for mosquitoes. Although a forest pond, the environment is marine-like.

Country Pond is frozen about four months out of the year, from mid-December to mid-April. Snowfall is frequent and accumulates to two to three feet on the ground. The spring thaw makes the level of the pond rise several feet. From May to November, a rowboat or canoe is the best way to explore the pond, to hug its jagged shore and explore inlets of marsh and cane. This was the way of the past, when Native American and white hunters traversed the pond by birch-bark canoe and trod the woods with snowshoes. Beaver, mink, lynx, bear, deer, moose, and wolves were plentiful. After 1800, as the population of New England grew because of natural increases and immigration, more people came to New Hampshire leaving behind the crowds of southern New England. A few reclusive souls sought out this lonely pond situated in-between the towns of Kingston, Newton, and Plaistow. Fishing shacks and woodworker's shops turned, by 1900, into summer camps for those from Haverhill and other Massachusetts cities looking for an escape into the country. In recent years the summer camps have given way to year-round residences.

This modest pond is now surrounded not only by the tall pines but numerous houses as well. Most are suburban residences that are narrow but several stories high, trying to make the most of limited space amid the dense forest. Roofs are covered with pine needles. Islands of concrete sporadically replace the virgin soil of the New England forest. In some places the stony ground has been worked into plush lawns surrounded by ornate fences. Boats not in the water or tied to the wharf are dry-docked, overturned, and resting on wooden stilts. Every residence has a wharf where during summer all manner of boats are moored. For a small body of water, Country Pond hosts speed boats, pontoon boats, ski boats, even the occasional seaplane.

Even so, the visitor to Country Pond tends to be blinded to the signs of modern progress and material ostentation, seeing only the sunlight piercing the swaying white pines, the ubiquitous pine-needles covering the ground, driving away grass, the old stone walls from another century, the deep verdure bogs in the forest, and the beautiful blue water of a pond on a sunny New England day.

Likewise New Hampshire attracts both visitor and resident not because of its busy highways, burgeoning technology, party atmosphere, elegant restaurants, expensive shops, and tourist traps. Rather New Hampshire attracts because of the daunting peaks of the north country, the endless stands of white pine and paper birch, the crystal streams alive with cold and newness, the rank salt marshes, hidden ponds, salty sea breeze, sandy beaches, and islands off the coast floating in the sea. But more, New Hampshire invites because, amid all the signs of modernity and progress, noise and activity, the roars of motorcycles and hum of traffic, there is the past, the ubiquitous sense of "what was." New Hampshire wears its heart on its sleeve, as it were. The heart of New Hampshire is its colonial heritage, when men and women crossed the ocean from England and elsewhere searching for a new life and finding it in a plentiful land that could not quite be tamed by the axe and the plow. Nature dominates in New Hampshire. This is what Robert Frost knew, and he expressed it over and over in his verse. Henry David Thoreau knew it as well, as he chronicled in his journey up the Merrimack River. Jeremy Belknap also knew it, as his *History of New-Hampshire* revealed. Neither Frost, Thoreau, nor Belknap were natives of New Hampshire, yet New Hampshire helped to mold their thoughts and writings. This is, perhaps, the real secret of New Hampshire. A person who visits does not want to leave, and even if he does the land has altered him in a way that cannot be expressed. Captain John Smith put it best when he sailed along the coast of New Hampshire in 1614. "This is onely as God made it, when he created the worlde."

Sources

Beals, Charles E. *Passaconaway in the White Mountains*. Boston: Richard G. Badger, 1916.

Beckey, Fred. *Mountains of North America*. San Francisco: Sierra Club Books, 1982.

Beebe, Richard W. *The First 200 Years: The History of the First Congregational Church*. Fryeburg, ME: Walker's Pond Press, 1975.

Bigelow, Jacob. "Some Account of the White Mountains of New Hampshire." *The New England Journal of Medicine and Surgery*. 5 (January, 1816).

Belknap, Jeremy. *The History of New Hampshire*. 3 vols. Philadelphia and Boston: Robert Aitken, Thomas and Andrews, Belknap and Young, 1784, 1791, 1792.

Bouton, Nathaniel. ed. *Documents and Records Relating to the Province of New-Hampshire*. Vol. 1 Concord: George Jenks, 1867.

——. *The History of Concord*. Concord: B. W. Sanborn, 1856.

Burt, F. Allen. *The Story of Mount Washington*. Hanover: Dartmouth Publications, 1960.

Clark, Charles E. *The Eastern Frontier: The Settlement of Northern New England, 1610–1763*. Hanover: University Press of New England, 1983.

Cutler, William P. and Julia P. Cutler, eds. *Life, Journals, and Correspondence of Rev. Manasseh Cutler, LL.D*. 2 vols. Cincinnati: Robert Clarke & Co., 1888.

Daniell, Jere R. *Colonial New Hampshire: A History*. Millwood, NY: KTO Press, 1981.

"Diaries of the Rev. Timothy Walker." In *Collections of the New Hampshire Historical Society*. Vol. 9 Concord.: Ira Evans, 1889.

Dwight, Timothy. *Travels, In New England and New-York*, 1821–1822.

Eastman, Benjamin. *North Conway: Its Surroundings, Its Settlement by English People*. North Conway: Reporter Press, n. d.

English, J. S. Indian Legends of the White Mountains. Boston: Rand Avery Supply Co., 1915.

Evans, George C. *History of the Town of Jefferson, New Hampshire, 1773–1927*. Manchester: Granite State Press, 1927.

Evans, George Hill. *Pigwacket. Part 1: Old Indian Days in the Valley of the Saco*. Conway: New Hampshire Historical Society, 1939.

Garvin, Donna-Belle and James L. Garvin. *On the Road North of Boston: New Hampshire Taverns and Turnpikes, 1700–1900*. Concord: New Hampshire Historical Society, 1988.

Hawthorne, Nathaniel. *The America Notebooks*. Columbus: Ohio State University Press, 1997.

Hosmer, James K. ed. *Winthrop's Journal: "History of New England," 1630–1649.* 2 vols. New York: Charles Scribner's Sons, 1908.

Hubbard, William. *General History of New England. In Collections of the Massachusetts Historical Society.* Series 2, Volumes 5 & 6. Boston: Massachusetts Historical Society, 1815; reprint ed. New York: Johnson Reprint Corp., 1968.

Jordan, Chester B. *Colonel Joseph B. Whipple.* Concord: Republican Press Association, 1894.

Josselyn, John. *New-Englands Rarities Discovered.* London: G. Widdowes, 1672.

Keyes, Donald D., et al. *The White Mountains: Place and Perceptions.* Hanover: University Press of New England, 1980.

Kilbourne, Frederick W. *Chronicles of the White Mountains.* New York: Houghton Mifflin Co., 1916.

Kirsch, George B. *Jeremy Belknap: A Biography.* New York: Arno Press, 1982.

Lawson, Russell M. *Passaconaway's Realm: Captain John Evans and the Exploration of Mount Washington.* Hanover, NH: University Press of New England, 2002.

—-. *Portsmouth: An Old Town by the Sea.* Charlestown, SC: Arcadia Publishing, 2003.

—-. *The American Plutarch: Jeremy Belknap and the Historian's Dialogue with the Past.* Westport: Praeger Publishers, 1998.

Lindholdt, Paul, ed. *John Josselyn, Colonial Traveler: A Critical Edition of Two Voyages to New-England.* Hanover: University Press of New England, 1988.

McDuffee, Franklin. *History of Rochester.* Vol. 1. Manchester: J. B. Clarke, 1892.

Merrill, Georgia. *History of Coos County.* Syracuse: WA: Fergusson and Co., 1888.

Ridlon, G. T. *Saco Valley Settlements and Families.* Self-published, Portland, ME, 1895.

Rogers, Robert. *A Concise Account of North America.* London: J. Millan 1765.

—-. *Reminiscences of the French War.* Freedom, N. H.: Freedom Historical Society, 1988.

Ross, William E., and Thomas M. House. *Durham: A Century in Photographs.* Dover, NH: Arcadia Publishing, 1996.

Stark, Caleb. ed. *Memoir and Official Correspondence of Gen. John Stark . . .* Boston: Gregg Press, 1972.

Thomas, Matthew. *Rockingham County.* Augusta, ME: Alan Sutton, 1994.

Varrell, William. *Rye and Rye Beach.* Dover, NH: Arcadia Publishing, 1995.

Waterman, Laura and Guy Waterman. *Forest and Crag: A History of Hiking, Trail Blazing, and Adventure in the Northeast Mountains.* Boston: Appalachian Mountain Club, 1989.

Whipple, Joseph. *The History of Acadie, Penobscot Bay and River.* Bangor: Peter Edes, 1816.

Willey, Benjamin G. *Incidents in White Mountain History.* Boston: Noyes, 1856.

Chronology of Major Events

1603	Martin Pring's journey up the Piscataqua River
1605	Samuel de Champlain's journey along the New Hampshire coast
1614	Captain John Smith's voyage along the New Hampshire coast
1632	Possible first ascent of Mount Washington
1623	Town of Dover founded
1635	Death of New Hampshire proprietor Captain John Mason
1638	Town of Hampton founded
1638	Rev. John Wheelright founds Exeter, New Hampshire
1642	Darby Field's ascent of Mount Washington
1652	Ascent of Merrimack River by Jonathan Ince and John Sherman
1679	Dominion of New England established
1697	Hannah Dustin kills and scalps Native American captors, escapes and descends Merrimack River returning home to Haverhill, Mass.
1725	Ascent of Mount Washington by Captain Wells
1728	Birth of John Stark at Derryfield
1732	Town of Durham founded
1741	Benning Wentworth becomes governor of NH
1764	Founding of Lancaster
1770	Darmouth College founded
1771	Timothy Nash's journey through the Crawford Notch
1774	Fort William and Mary stormed by colonials led by John Sullivan and John Langdon
1778	New Hampshire towns of the Connecticut Valley declare themselves independent
1781	Phillips-Exeter Academy founded at Exeter
1782	Birth of Daniel Webster at Franklin
1783	New Hampshire state constitution ratified
1784	Belknap/Cutler Expedition to the White Mountains
1784	Publication of the first volume of Jeremy Belknap's *History of New-Hampshire*
1786	Discontented farmers march on Exeter and are dispersed by John Sullivan
1788	New Hampshire is the ninth and deciding state to ratify the Constitution
1782	Establishment of Canterbury Shaker Village
1800	Founding of Portsmouth Naval Shipyard
1804	Manasseh Cutler's Ascent of Mount Washington
1816	Ascent of Mount Washington by Jacob Bigelow

1816	Concord becomes capitol of New Hampshire
1819	State House built at Concord
1826	Landslide kills Willey family living at Crawford Notch
1831	Amoskeag Manufacturing Company founded at Manchester
1842	Webster–Ashburton Treaty settles boundary between New Hampshire and Canada
1847	Ten hour workday mandated by New Hampshire state legislature
1853	Franklin Pierce becomes president of the United States
1861	Carriage road to summit of Mount Washington built
1866	Founding of the University of New Hampshire
1869	Cog railway to summit of Mount Washington completed
1893	New Hampshire law requires a public library in each town
1905	Wreck of the *Lizzie Carr* along the New Hampshire coast
1905	Theodore Roosevelt hosts peace conference at Portsmouth that ends Russo-Japanese War
1907	Founding of MacDowell Colony for artists at Peterborough
1920	New Hampshire presidential primary held before any other state primaries
1923	Publication of Robert Frost's poem, "New Hampshire"
1928	Baker Library at Dartmouth College built
1932	Highest wind speed ever recorded atop Mount Washington
1936	Close of Amoskeag Manufacturing Company of Manchester
1944	International Monetary Fund created at United Nations conference meeting at Bretton Woods.
1961	New Hampshire native Alan Shepard first American in space
1964	State lottery created to help fund public education
1986	Space shuttle *Challenger* disaster kills New Hampshire teacher Christa McAuliffe
1997	New Hampshire Supreme Court rules in the "Claremont case" that property taxes cannot be used to fund public education
1999	New Hampshire the fiftieth state to enact the Martin Luther King holiday
2003	V. Gene Robinson, openly-homosexual, becomes Ninth Episcopal Bishop of New Hampshire

CULTURAL HIGHLIGHTS

WRITERS

Aldrich, Thomas Bailey, novelist, author of *The Story of a Bad Boy*
Clark, Charles, historian, author of *Eastern Frontier*
Daniell, Jere, historian, author of *Colonial New Hampshire*
Doan, Daniel, nature writer and historian, author of *Indian Stream Republic*
Eberhart, Richard, poet, author of Pulitzer Prize-winning *Selected Poems*
Frost, Robert, New Hampshire's greatest poet
Heald, Bruce, local historian, author of numerous books on local New Hampshire history
Hebert, Ernest, novelist, author of *The Old American*
Huntington, Cynthia, NH Poet Laureate, author of *The Radiant*
Randall, Peter, publisher, author of *New Hampshire: A Living Landscape*
Roberts, Kenneth, historical novelist, author of *Northwest Passage*
Rule, Rebecca, novelist, author of *The Best Revenge*
Starbuck, David, historian, author of *The Shaker Family Album*
Thaxter, Celia, poet and writer, author of *Among the Isles of Shoals*
Tolles, Bryant, architectural historian, author of *New Hampshire Architecture*
Wetherell, W. D., writer, author of *This American River*

MOVIES

Hotel New Hampshire (1984): story of a family who lives in a renovated NH hotel
Northwest Passage (1940): tale of Robert Rogers of New Hampshire
On Golden Pond (1982): filmed on location at Squam Lake

PLAYS

The God Who Made New Hampshire, by Joe Lauinger
Our Town, by Thornton Wilder

MUSIC

Evensong, duo, Exeter
New Hampshire Symphony Orchestra, Manchester
The Shaw Brothers, folk duo

Special Events

An Evening of Dance, Keene State College, Keene
Art 'Round Town, monthly, Portsmouth
Candlelight Stroll, December, Portsmouth
Celebrity Series (music, dance, plays), University of New
    Hampshire, Durham
Exeter Revolutionary War Festival, July, Exeter
Francestown Contra Dances, monthly, Francestown
Hanover Street Fest, July, Hanover
League of New Hampshire Craftsmen's Fair, August, Newbury
Mount Washington Auto Road annual birthday celebration,
    August, Gorham
Mount Washington Auto Road Bicycle Hill Climb, August,
    Gorham
New England 300 NASCAR race, July, Loudon
New Hampshire Highland Games, September, Hopkinton
Prescott Park Arts Festival, June–August, Portsmouth
Portsmouth Maritime Folk Festival, September, Portsmouth
Stratham Fair, July, Stratham

Contact Information

New Hampshire Department of Cultural Resources, 20 Park St.
    Concord, NH 03301 (603-271-2540)
New Hampshire Historical Society, 30 Park St., Concord, NH
    03301 (603-228-6688) www.visitnh.gov
New Hampshire Public Radio, 207 N. Main St. Concord, NH
    03301 (603-228-8910)
New Hampshire State Council on the Arts, Concord, NH 03301
    (603-271-2789)
New Hampshire State Library, 20 Park St., Concord, NH 03301
    (603-271-2144)
New Hampshire Writer's Project, P. O Box 2693, Concord, NH
    03302 (603-226-6649)
Office of Travel and Tourism, P. O. Box 1856, Concord, NH
    03302 (800-386-4664);
White Mountain National Forest, P. O. Box 638, Laconia, NH
    03247 (877-444-6777)

Further Reading

Websites

New Hampshire Almanac (at www.state.nh.us/nhinfo):
    information on history and government
New Hampshire Guidebook, annual (at www.visitnh.gov)
    www.NH.com: New Hampshire news.
www.NHEvents.com: yearly arts, town, historical events.
www.NHMagazine.com: articles and state profiles
www.nhoutdoors.com: information on outdoor activities and sports
www.nhpr.org: NH public radio website
www.seacoastnh.com: links to Seacoast history and activities.
www.summertheatre.com: information on NH summer theatre
www.visitnh.gov: website on events and tourism

Books

AMC White Mountain Guide. Boston: Appalachian Mountain
    Club, 2003.
Clark, Charles. *The Eastern Frontier: The Settlement of Northern
    New England, 1610–1763*. Hanover, NH: University Press of
    New England, 1983.
Daniell, Jere. *Colonial New Hampshire: A History*. Millwood, NY:
    KTO Press, 1981.
Doan, Daniel. *Fifty Hikes in the White Mountains*. Woodstock,
    VT: Countryman Press, 2000.
——. *Fifty More Hikes in New Hampshire*. Woodstock, VT:
    Countryman Press, 1991.
Garvin, Donna-Belle, and James L. Garvin. *On the Road North of
    Boston: New Hampshire Taverns and Turnpikes, 1700–1900*.
    Concord, NH: New Hampshire Historical Society, 1988.
Lawson, Russell. *Passaconaway's Realm: Captain John Evans and
    the Exploration of Mount Washington*. Hanover, NH:
    University Press of New England, 2002.
——. *Portsmouth: An Old Town by the Sea*. Charlestown, SC:
    Arcadia Publishing, 2003.
Wilderson, Paul. *Governor John Wentworth and the American
    Revolution*. Hanover, NH: University Press of New
    England, 1994.